The Economic Life of the Ancient World

The Economic Life of the Ancient World

Jean-Philippe Lévy

Translated by John G. Biram

The University of Chicago Press/Chicago & London

Title-page illustrations: Two sides of a Greek coin, one bearing a portrait of Demetrius, king of Bactria (*ca.* 190–160 B.C.), and the other a representation of Zeus and the inscription "King Demetrius." Reproduced by permission of the Trustees of the British Museum.

Originally published in 1964 as L' économie antique *© 1964, Presses Universitaires de France*

Chronology and enlarged bibliography were prepared for the English edition by the author

Library of Congress Catalog Card Number: 67–20575

THE UNIVERSITY OF CHICAGO PRESS, CHICAGO & LONDON
The University of Toronto Press, Toronto 5, Canada

Published 1967
Printed in the United States of America

Preface

During prehistoric times, man had already made some fundamental progress in technology: domestication of certain animals, cultivation of land, weaving, pottery, metallurgy of copper and gold, and navigation. His economic activity, however, was quite restricted at the time when history can properly be said to begin, a time which varied with the society in question.

If, at the end of the period of ancient history, we consider the economic situation along the banks of the Seine or the Rhine some time after the fall of the Roman Empire, it is almost possible to believe that this primitive stage of development had scarcely been superseded. Between these two extreme limits, however, the economy had gone through a remarkable peak of development lasting several centuries and had attained a level which it was barely able to recover in the West prior to the last centuries of the Middle Ages.

It is this evolution that we propose to study, and we shall do so within a geographical framework limited to the periphery of the Mediterranean, varying in extent from region to region. This whole area is the cradle of the civilization from which our own has grown. We shall ignore not only peoples of prehistoric times but also the Far East, except in regard to its infrequent contacts with the West.

Our study will be divided into four chapters corresponding to the major phases of the general history of the period, whose key points are the military victories of Alexander, the establishment of the Roman Empire after the Battle of Actium, and the onset of its dissolution during the third century A.D.

Contents

CHAPTER ONE

THE GRAECO-ORIENTAL WORLD BEFORE ALEXANDER 1

I. General Conditions and Primitive Form of the Economy in Ancient Times 1
- A. Primitive Agriculture
- B. General Conditions Relating to Industry
- C. Distribution, Exchange, and Commerce

II. Two Great Economic Powers: Egypt and Mesopotamia 7
- A. The Egyptian System of Control of the Economy
- B. The Babylonian Money-making Outlook

III. Maritime and Colonial Expansion of the Phoenicians and Greeks 10
- A. The Phoenicians
- B. The Greeks

IV. The First Appearance of Money 14
- A. The Premonetary Stage
- B. Money

V. The Economy in Classical Greece 22
- A. The Rapid Progress of Commerce
- B. Effects on Production
- C. Social Consequences

CHAPTER TWO

THE HELLENISTIC ERA 33

I. THE HELLENISTIC AND CARTHAGINIAN WORLD 33
A. The General Conditions of Hellenistic Economics
B. The Decline of Greece
C. The Egyptian State-controlled Economy
D. Carthaginian Isolation

II. ROMAN PENETRATION INTO THE HELLENISTIC ECONOMY 46
A. Economic Antecedents in Italy up to the Third Century B.C.
B. The Integration of Rome in the Hellenistic Economic Life
C. Exploitation of Conquest
D. Repercussions in Italy

CHAPTER THREE

THE EARLY ROMAN EMPIRE (LE HAUT-EMPIRE) 71

I. THE ECONOMIC APOGEE 71
A. Commercial Expansion
B. The Progress of Agriculture
C. Industry

II. ECONOMIC AND GEOGRAPHICAL IMBALANCES 76
A. Imbalance between Production and Consumption
B. Geographical Imbalance
C. Imbalance of Trade with the Far East

III. INTERNAL TRANSFORMATIONS 80
A. Tendency toward Business Mergers
B. Changes in the Status of Farm Laborers
C. Development of Corporative Bodies

CHAPTER FOUR

THE LATER ROMAN EMPIRE 84

I. THE ECONOMIC CRISIS 84
A. Crisis in Agricultural Production

B. Monetary Crisis
C. Crisis in Circulation and Exchange
D. Crisis in the Distribution of Wealth
II. The Planned Economy 92
A. Regulation of the Economy
B. Direct State Intervention
C. Professional and Corporate Organizations

CONCLUSION 101
CHRONOLOGY 105
BIBLIOGRAPHY 115
INDEX 141

CHAPTER ONE

The Graeco-Oriental World before Alexander

The primitive type of economic system was, in the main, maintained over a long period. But against this general background, two regions stand out clearly as early as the third millennium: Egypt and Mesopotamia. Next began the maritime expansion of the Phoenicians, and then of the Greeks, at the start of the first millennium. This brought on a real revolution, marked by the first appearance of money. Finally, in the fifth and fourth centuries B.C., Greece made new advances. These are the successive stages of this prolonged period.

I. GENERAL CONDITIONS AND PRIMITIVE FORM OF THE ECONOMY IN ANCIENT TIMES

A. Primitive Agriculture

In the ancient economic system, agriculture predominated and was the source of the chief forms of wealth. But in speaking of agriculture, one must include the pastoral economy which preceded it, and whose importance is very great. There were pastoral peoples and nomads, like the Bedouins and the Hebrew patriarchs. Even non-nomadic groups had huge flocks and herds. In the *Iliad,* a husband offers his wife 100 oxen, 1,000 goats, and 1,000 lambs, showing that he had an immense fortune in livestock. Furthermore, some societies which remained temporarily settled would become nomadic from time to time, and these large-scale migrations resulted in their moving en masse from one habitat to another. Besides stock-raising, forestry economy also had an importance which it has lost in our era.

In regard to agricultural economy in the proper sense of the term, the crop cultivated obviously varied widely, but the area which formed the Graeco-Oriental world practiced three basic forms of cultivation. The first was grain, which supplied the main foodstuff: above all barley, and wheat somewhat later on; then the vine, very widespread around the Mediterranean, and also fruit trees, almost all originating in Asia. Finally, oleaginous plants supplied not only edible oil but also oil for lighting and for toilet uses. The olive was widespread in Greece, Syria and Palestine. In Egypt oleaginous-grain crops were grown; sesame, castor-oil plants, croton, and so forth.

We may ask what was the system under which agriculture was carried out—collective or private ownership. This was debated in vain at the beginning of our century. It is certainly necessary here to distinguish between one society and another. One would clear an area of land, cultivate it for a time, and abandon it at the first sign of it becoming exhausted. Others, like the Greeks, were familiar with at least family ownership if not individual private property. The agricultural unit so constituted was more or less self-governing and strove to be self-sufficient: one must nevertheless not exaggerate the exclusive character of this closed domestic economy.

Agricultural techniques were very rudimentary. Ploughs were wooden and without wheels, often without mouldboard. They were yoked to oxen or mules, never to horses. The crop was harvested with reaping hooks to avoid loss of grain. The grain was ground in a mortar with a pestle or with a millstone driven by slaves or donkeys. There was no fertilizer. In general, land was fallowed biennially, that is, left untilled one year in every two.

B. General Conditions Relating to Industry

Although the term "industry" seems out of keeping with the scale of manufacture in these remote times, it will be used for want of a better. In the main, there were four kinds. Firstly, construction of houses, palaces, fortresses, dikes, and bridges, not forgetting shipbuilding; then clothes and carpets; pottery; and lastly, metallurgy. The last-named is subdivided into three: manufacture of tools (for agriculture or the smithy); weapons and shields for warfare; luxury items in jewelry or furniture (vases, tripods, and so forth). These types of manufacture appeared in what has been called "the first industrial revolution," which occurred at the end of prehistoric times.

Many of the principal materials were indigenous and local: ordinary stone, clay, textiles, hides, and skins. This was even more often the case with timber, but certain countries (Egypt, Mesopotamia) had virtually none, and some woods were much sought after, such as the cedar of Lebanon or of the Amanus Mountains, which explains transportation over great distances. Other raw materials were always sought far and wide: precious stones or gemstones, and above all, metals, transported either as minerals or as artifacts.

Metalworking of gold and silver dates back to prehistoric times. This is also true for unalloyed copper, which yields only mediocre products. One great invention was bronze (copper alloyed with tin), which first appeared in the area around Susa (eastern Mesopotamia) in the third millennium B.C. It was unknown in Egypt until the following millennium. The search for minerals gave rise to sizable expeditions. The chief copper mines were in Cyprus (whence the name "copper") and on the Sinai peninsula. Tin, a very rare metal, came from the Caucasus or the mysterious Cassiterides islands, perhaps in fact those off the southwest point of England (the Scillies).

Iron was the last to appear. Its ore is very widely distributed, but metal extraction is difficult. It is curious that, in all the regions known, the metallurgy of iron first originates in the northern part: the Hyksos in Egypt, the Dorians in Greece, and the Gauls in France without doubt owed their victories to their long iron swords. Perhaps we are dealing here with an Indo-European invention. But iron remained scarce and valuable. In the time of Hammurabi, it was eight times more costly than copper in Babylon. A few centuries later, a pharaoh of the Eighteenth Dynasty asked his ally, the Hittite king, to send him a gift made of iron; the king sent him a simple iron dagger, apologizing for having nothing better. In the *Iliad,* the victor in a discus contest carries off as his prize the iron disc he has thrown, and Akhilleus remarks that this would be enough to supply the needs of a large estate for five years. Egypt only really passed into the Iron Age during the first millennium B.C. The most civilized peoples were thus still in the Bronze Age.

Industrial technology was as yet very primitive. There was no motive force other than animal. Human manual labor alone was used; furthermore it was very plentiful and dirt-cheap.

Although it is true that many things, especially clothes, were made at home by the consumers themselves (Odysseus and Penelope made bed, boat, and fabrics by hand), building, pottery, and metalwork were almost entirely concentrated in the hands of professional artisans. The mines were often state enterprises, thanks to slave labor or military expeditions.

C. Distribution, Exchange, and Commerce

German economic historians have distinguished three successive stages in the evolution of the economy. The oldest is supposed to have been the domestic (*Hauswirtschaft*), with virtually no division of labor, producers and consumers being almost one and the same, and hence no commerce. The next stage is said to have been one of urban economy (*Stadtwirtschaft*), where producers sold their products directly to the consumers without middlemen. The last stage was called worldwide economy (*Weltwirtschaft*), i.e., an international commerce and credit system.

In reality, and in opposition to what the inventors of this classification have thought, international trade dates back to the dawn of history but—and this is very important and often lost sight of—for a very long time it dealt only with very few items, essentially of three kinds: luxury items, high value for low weight, such as gems, spices (incense, aromatics, perfume), ivory, purple, or purple-dyed fabrics, sometimes rare animals (monkeys, peacocks); then, slaves; finally minerals (including rock salt) or metals, which must be transported since they can only be taken from where Nature put them. All other merchandise gave rise to purely local trade. Large-scale trade in foodstuffs did not exist in antiquity: it only appeared much later and was quite rare throughout ancient times.

1. DISTRIBUTION, TRANSPORTATION

Long-distance transportation had three possible routes: overland, river, and maritime. Land transportation was carried out on the backs of men or animals for a long time. Roads only appeared in Mesopotamia after 3000 B.C., and in Egypt with the Hyksos. Asses and oxen were the animals used. The camel, long known in Asia, only became widespread in Egypt in our own epoch (A.D.). The horse, called the "mountain ass" by the Babylonians and the "animal of the East" by the Hittites, appeared late and may have been introduced by the Indo-Europeans. Some monuments of the Minoan era depict their historic disembarkation in Crete.

They only came into general use in the thirteenth century B.C., but mainly for military purposes. They could not pull heavy loads or ploughs because, until the end of the period of antiquity, no one knew the techniques of shoeing or harnessing. Land transportation was also undeveloped, although certain routes were already set up with intermittent caravanserais, water-storage cisterns, and guard posts to ensure the safety of travelers.

Since the most remote times, rivers such as the Nile and the Euphrates had been used for transportation. Others, like the Tigris, were too swift running and were only used in the downstream direction. A boat was built, loaded, and floated down river; on arrival the cargo was sold along with the boat, whose timber was a valuable material.

Despite the great perils of navigation, the beginnings of maritime transportation are lost in the dim and distant past. The oldest and greatest trade route in the world is the Red Sea, extending beyond it along the coastline of Arabia and into the Persian gulf: the mariners of protohistory used this route to put Egypt and Mesopotamia in contact with Africa and India. Boats were plying the Mediterranean at least 2,000 years before the Christian era. Their construction made continuous progress—ships were described as "of Byblos," then "of Crete," then "of Tarshish," * the name of the town in southern Spain reached by the Phoenicians in traveling the whole length of the Mediterranean and perhaps even braving the Atlantic ocean.

The idea of cutting a canal through the isthmus of Suez goes back at least to the Twelfth Dynasty of Egypt, which may perhaps have been responsible for it. The canal was certainly operational during the Nineteenth Dynasty. It was dredged and enlarged around 600 B.C. by Necho [or Necoh], and then by Darius. But this canal, which joined the eastern branch of the Nile to the Bitter Lakes, never played more than a minor role.

* I Kings 10:22 and 22:48.—TRANSLATOR'S NOTE.

2. METHODS OF COMMERCE

The primitive forms of international trade did not always presuppose the existence of specialist merchants. It has been said that the earliest form of trade was piracy and that it was this, rather than war, which provided most of the slaves, captured in raids. A second form of trade was the military expedition. The earliest pharaohs organized expeditions to the copper mines of Sinai, expelled the Bedawi of the region by force, seized some of the ore, and returned to Egypt. Finally trade assumed the form of diplomacy, by exchange of gifts or payment of tribute; and this was how the New Empire of Egypt traded with all her neighbors, near or far, as far away as the Hittites and the "land of Cush" (present-day Ethiopia). These methods required no money (other than gifts) as a medium of exchange.

II. TWO GREAT ECONOMIC POWERS: EGYPT AND MESOPOTAMIA

By virtue of their power and technological innovations, Egypt and Mesopotamia stand out clearly against the general background from the third millennium onward. This they owed to their large-scale agricultural productivity, a new phenomenon in that it was enough to ensure the food supply of very important towns whose inhabitants were not farmers. Egypt was "the gift of the Nile." It possessed all the ingredients of fertility: its famous black soil, sun, and water from the midsummer flooding. Mesopotamia's prosperity was also considerable but less stable, since the flooding of its two rivers (in spring) is short-lived and very violent. There was a risk of the countryside being devastated, and in our time the area has become largely desert.

A. The Egyptian System of Control of the Economy

The exceptional fertility of Egypt depended on human cooperation. Immense engineering constructions had to be built and constantly renovated to retain water and alluvium. An emergency reservoir was created in the Twelfth Dynasty by making use of Lake Moeris, and the land recovered from the surrounding marshes formed the richest area of the country, el Fayum. It was likewise necessary to enact regulations for conservation of water, which was rationed. These requirements provide a partial explanation of the absolutism which was a characteristic of Egypt's political organization.

State control (or, since subtleties are of little importance, state planning or state socialism) was predominant here as a constant factor throughout the whole of the ancient history of Egypt. She was the oldest society to be organized on this principle. Everything emanated from the pharaoh or from his administration, and his subjects lived under a disciplinary regime, surrounded by officials, tax collectors, and overseers, with the ever present threat of the cudgel.

In addition to public works and regulations, the intervention of state power in economic life mainly resulted in her ownership of the means of production. Even if individual property, or that of temples or funeral institutions, was not unknown, the phrases "the king's land" and "the fields of Pharaoh" were frequently used. In certain periods the king also owned all professions and civil, military, and religious offices, which he distributed among his subjects. This whole system involved the drafting of inventories, registers of land surveys, incessant proclamations and censuses, and an army of scribes and accountants.

But the state did not only intervene in production. It directed distribution and consumption. It appropriated a fraction (usually large) of the harvest and hoarded it in warehouses, granaries, and depots situated even in the smallest villages or in "supply towns." The stores consisted of food, animals, cloth, metals, even furniture. These resources not only served to defray state expenses but also formed provisions for years of scarcity. The provident state laid up goods for its subjects. The king, it was said, is "he who presides over the food supplies of all," which is also shown by the Bible story of the seven lean kine. The distributions were made in a twofold spirit—desire for gain, and foresight or paternalism. The king sold dear what he had stored, but he and his administrators felt themselves duty bound to ensure the subsistence of everyone.

B. The Babylonian Money-making Outlook

Babylon, which differed from Egypt, had first of all an attitude exclusively concerned with wealth; also, individual initiative played a considerable part there.

Mesopotamia was one of the major trade routes of antiquity. Trade was very important and it was there that new phenomena emerged. First of all, there were professional traders who were not producers but dealt only with the products of others; and generally were great travelers, playing the part of middlemen exclusively. A system of weights (the talent or *kikkar* subdivided into 60 *minas* of 60 shekels) and measures was set up early, on a logical basis; this system was followed by most of the peoples of ancient times. Notaries established the formulation of various commercial contracts (sales, hiring, business partnerships), written on clay tablets and stamped with the seals of the contracting parties.

Equipped with these methods, commerce here soon reaped the benefits of developments far from Babylon. From the third millennium, Sumerian or Akkadian merchants became established in Cappadocia. It was only at sea that the Babylonians seemed seldom willing to take a risk. During a period of almost 2,000 years, Babylon was to be a famous commercial metropolis whose accursed memory is to be found in the Bible and even in the Book of Revelation.

Another remarkable feature here was the great mobility of capital. Temples and kings were large-scale capitalists, but there were numerous private individuals among them.[1] In-

[1] Such as the Murashu family, Nippur bankers of the fifth century B.C., which has been studied by my learned colleague M. Cardascia.

vestments were made first of all in agriculture: herds were bought, and also land, to be cultivated by wage earners or sharecroppers. Investments also took the form of loans, money or seed; the rate of interest was 20 per cent for money and 33 per cent for barley, so that the borrower, as well as his family, risked slavery for nonpayment of debt if he defaulted. The limited partnership was also a Babylonian invention: it allowed the sleeping [in American, "silent"] partner to find the business capital, in cash or goods, while the other worked and traveled.

III. MARITIME AND COLONIAL EXPANSION OF THE PHOENICIANS AND GREEKS

An event of considerable importance was to upset the prevailing economic conditions: the Phoenicians, prior to the year 1000 B.C., and the Greeks thereafter, enter the maritime and colonial epic story. Timid attempts had already been made previously by the Aegeans and Cretans, and later on by the Akhaians (or Achaeans) and Mycenaeans. The Trojan War was probably caused by rivalry between them and the Phrygians, who wanted to maintain control over passage through the straits. It may have been during this period that the legend of the Argonauts was born; the fabulous tale of an expedition to the Black Sea as far as Colchis, present-day Georgia. But these first attempts ended in failure due to the cataclysmic Dorian invasion. In the obscure period which followed, the Phoenicians obtained a monopoly of trade as far as the Aegean Sea, but were forced, little by little, to give way once more to the Greeks, who had recovered themselves in the interim.

In addition to trading, each group founded colonies, but there were two differences between their methods of expansion. All in all, the Phoenicians mainly peddled wares produced by others, while the Greeks carried their own goods and oriented their industry with a view to export. On the other hand, apart from Carthage (whose expansion was the last to take place), the Phoenicians had only ports and small settlements without hinterland, whereas the Greeks had large colonial settlements.

A. The Phoenicians

From before 2000 B.C., Byblos traded regularly with Egypt. The *floruit* of Ugarit was to come a few centuries later. Around 1000 B.C., these cities were in full decline, and the principal commercial cities were Sidon and, in particular, Tyre.

The basis of their powerful position was the cedar and fir forests of Lebanon and its northern extension, the Amanus Mountains, which supplied the timber for shipbuilding. Three millennia before the Dutch, the Phoenicians were the "carriers of the seas." Besides true commerce, they did not hesitate to practice piracy, especially with a view to capturing slaves: the *Odyssey* depicts them landing on an island, displaying their wares and drumming up customers, and while the local menfolk were absorbed in all this, a detachment of Phoenicians carried off the women and children to sell elsewhere. When the occasion demanded, however, they also knew how to behave themselves most correctly.

In those days it was rare for navigation to take place out of sight of land, and it was impossible at night. The Phoenicians therefore established closely spaced ports for their way stations, and the port became the center of a settlement. This was how their colonies originated. Nevertheless, some of these settlements did not amount to a whole town: they were satisfied with a street or a district, as at Memphis.

Although the Greeks recaptured control of the Aegean, Phoenician trade extended further and further west. Their ports were staged regularly, every 20 or 30 kilometers, the length of the African coast of the Mediterranean, where their largest colony, Carthage, was founded about 814 B.C. They spread as far as the Pillars of Melkarth (Straits of Gibraltar) and they had at Tarshish, in southern Spain, important establishments primarily devoted to metallurgy. From there they even launched out into the Atlantic and went to search for tin in the Cassiterides. They also colonized the western part of Sicily.

Some of their expeditions are famous. In the tenth century B.C. they organized a fleet for the benefit of King Solomon in the Gulf of 'Aqaba near the land of Ophir, ruled by the Queen of Sheba. Around 600 B.C. the Pharaoh Necho [or Necoh] sent them on a voyage of exploration lasting three years, starting from the Red Sea; and historians have wondered how much truth there is in the story that they told on their return, stating that they had circumnavigated the African continent and seen the sun rise first on their left, then on their right. A short time later, the Carthaginian admiral Hanno traveled by sea to the Gulf of Guinea.

Although less well known, and giving rise to no colonies, their land trade must have had a degree of importance, nevertheless. It was Hiram, king of Tyre, who supplied Solomon with the costliest materials of construction for the temple at Jerusalem, and an army of skilled workers.

After having peddled the products only of others over a long period, the Phoenicians set themselves to making their own wares for sale. But they had little originality and confined themselves to copying other peoples. For example, they imported pottery and crude little idols in Egyptian style which the Greeks called "pygmies." They did, however, invent two things: first, purple, extracted from a mollusc (murex), and also purple-dyed fabrics; second, glass, not opaque like the Egyptian, but transparent or stained (tinted), and from this they made objets d'art or the plain glassware that they sold to the barbarians.

B. The Greeks

At first the Greeks were cautious mariners, and not too sure of themselves; in Homeric times the Phoenicians were still their suppliers. Thereafter they made progress, and around 1000 B.C. they established themselves on the coast of Asia Minor. Further expansion came about from the eighth century B.C. onwards.

They had two types of colony. The oldest, established in fertile areas and sparsely populated at first, were aimed solely at agriculture. The others were straightforward trading settlements at the outlets of trade routes or on narrows. As time went by, the two types tended to merge and industry was added. It was in southern Italy and in Sicily, which came to be called "Magna Graecia," that the most important colonies were founded, in the eighth century B.C. at the latest. One of these, Syracuse, was to become one of the greatest cities of antiquity. Some others are also famous: Sybaris, and her victorious rival Croton; Tarentum; even a colony as far away as Cumae, an outpost toward the north beyond Naples. The route from Corinth to Corfu, Tarentum, Syracuse, and the Straits of Messina was one of the vital arteries of the Hellenic world. The Greeks fought for centuries with the Carthaginians over Sicily.

They also clashed with each other in the extreme western areas of the Mediterranean. There, the chief Greek colony was Massilia (founded by the Phocaeans [or Phokaians]), influential from the fourth century on. The Greeks also established themselves in the rich mining area of southern Spain near Tarshish, which they called "Tartessos." In 535 the naval battle of Alalia (present-day Aleria) took place off the coast of Corsica: both the Phoenicians and the Massiliots proclaimed themselves victors, but the latter evacuated Corsica.

Some Greek colonies were also established toward the northeast, along the straits and the shores of the Pontus Euxinus, where the cold, damp climate always hindered settlement; these colonies were hardly more than trade agencies, numerous and active. In the south, the Greeks had settlements in Cyprus, Cyrene, and Libya; and in the middle of the sixth century the Pharaoh Amasis gave them a special town—Naukratis, on the Nile delta.

This colonization caused the decline of the power of the Phoenicians, who were in competition and in combat with the Greeks; the former were forced to confine themselves to local transportation of goods along their own coast and Africa's. This set off a new and genuine economic revolution; first in agriculture, by bringing new, very fertile land into production, especially in Magna Graecia; then in industry, which was thus able to find abundant raw materials and markets; lastly, and most important of all, in distribution of goods. From this time on, and for the first time in history, we see trade and transportation of heavy goods * destined for human consumption or use in industry: wine, oil, dried or salted fish, wheat, timber, wool, and hides. Without doubt this trade was very limited in extent, but its significance was to increase appreciably in the fifth century. Greek maritime expansion thus opened the door to world, or at the very least, to international economics; and the Greeks had customers who were Greek or barbarians (Scythians, Ligurians, Iberians, Gauls) all around the Mediterranean basin.

IV. THE FIRST APPEARANCE OF MONEY

In our times, money is only symbolic. It was originally a commodity and long remained so. On the other hand, the different functions of money, which we have a tendency to confuse today, remained distinct for a considerable period. What is properly described as payment money or real money is the object (coin, or nowadays the bill) that is actually handed over at the time of payment. Nominal money is a purely auditing or legal concept that states the amount of a debt or compares values—it provides a common standard of measurement. Finally, money is also a means of saving or hoarding. According to the role it has to play, this special commodity, money, must exhibit certain characteristics. For nominal money one needs a commodity both very well known

* Generally defined as weighing more than a thousand kilograms per cubic meter.—TRANSLATOR'S NOTE.

and constant in value, although there is no need for it to be given an intrinsic value. Real money must be easy to handle, to carry around, and thus to be identifiable from three angles: nature, quality, weight. Finally, savings money cannot be any perishable item.

The metal coin, which combines all these qualities, did not appear until quite late: very active trading civilizations (such as the Babylonians and Phoenicians) were able to arise, without money proper, in a premonetary system.

A. The Premonetary Stage

The first procedure, historically speaking, was obviously barter or exchange (as opposed to buying and selling) of one object for another, without the use of money: we are thus speaking of "natural" and nonmonetary economy. Barter pure and simple is very awkward, however: the two objects offered in mutual exchange may not be mutually acceptable; and above all, how is one to fix their relative values? However far back one goes in history, the primitive stage (which may be considered as monetary prehistory) where barter alone prevails, is either superseded, or is only discovered in exceptional cases such as that of trade between peoples who had no regular contact with one another.[2] Elsewhere, people had thought of facilitating exchange by using a third commodity as an intermediary device. This brings us at once to the protohistory of money. The series of tentative efforts that men made here gave rise to three principal practices, sometimes found all together, and it is hard to date the first appearances of each separate one.

1. Nominal Money

Money acting only as an accounting device, not for payment, was in existence in Egypt in the Fourth or Fifth Dy-

[2] Such as the well-known trade between Carthaginians and African Negroes (Herodotus IV, 196: low-quality wares were exchanged for powdered gold). See also *Iliad* VII, 472 ff.

nasty, in the first centuries of the third millennium. The scribe Thenti sold his house to the priest Kemapu. The house was valued at ten *shats,* a term apparently signifying a ring of gold weighing about 7.5 grams. But this ring was not given to the seller: Kemapu paid Thenti in items of furniture and fabrics valued respectively at 4, 3, and 3 *shats.* Many analogous contracts will have occurred in the New Empire (fourteenth century) and up to the Twenty-sixth Dynasty (seventh century): animals, clothes, land, and days of labor were exchanged after evaluation in weight of gold, or silver, which was purely nominal money.

2. NONMETALLIC MONEY

Another practice just as ancient was to use as nominal money, or nominal and real simultaneously, a current nonmetallic commodity, approximately constant in value. The one most frequently used was grain. This has been found in Egypt and Babylonia: pictographic documents prior to the invention of cuneiform writing, dating back perhaps to the fourth millennium, depict the ideas of price and purchase by the sketch of a bag of grain. The codes drafted around 2000 B.C. used barley to fix the price of goods, rents, and wages, but at this period barley was already in competition with silver and relationships or equivalents between them are provided.

Although their value was much less stable, animals have acted as money, but more rarely; this was particularly the case with the Greeks and Romans. In the *Iliad,* objects offered to victors at the games—tripod, cauldron, armor—were valued at 12, 1, 9, and 100 oxen. A slave was worth 4 to 20. Dowries and ransoms were paid in oxen. We shall see similar practices in ancient Rome. These forms of money (perishables) have the considerable inconvenience of being quite unsuitable for saving.

3. NONMONETARY METAL

This practice accounts for the success of metal (as money). The nonmonetary metal economy goes back a long time. Gold has been used in all periods, but very rarely; silver in Mesopotamia; copper and bronze in Egypt; a curiosity, and a relic of the period when it was expensive, was the use of iron in Sparta. But metal did not yet take the form of a coin; it went by weight, or was measured out, or, at most, was stamped.

Metal could be paid out in any form which came to hand: ingot, bar, grain, or as various objects. A series of verification processes had to precede payment: ringing, testing by touchstone, to tell the kind and grade of metal; and objects were weighed. In Mesopotamia, silver was used this way from the third millennium up to the fifth, perhaps even to the third century B.C.; the unit of weight was the shekel, which was just over 8 grams. According to Genesis (23:16), when Abraham bought the cave of Machpelah from Ephron the Hittite to bury his wife Sarah: "Abraham weighed unto Ephron the silver which he had named in the audience of the sons of Heth, 400 shekels of silver, current money with the merchant." This weighing of silver turns up again in Jerusalem at the beginning of the sixth century B.C. (Jer. 32:9–10). Most coinages kept the name of a weight: shekel, *mina* (60 shekels), and talent (60 *minas*) in the East; the *stater* (etymology: "weighing") among the Greeks; not to mention the pound of modern or contemporary countries.

To avoid weighing or proving the metal, various advances were gradually made. It may be that certain peoples, such as the Greeks of Asia, used preweighed metals to avoid having to weigh it, and paid with current utensils (tripods, cauldrons, brooches, axes, rings). It appears possible that the Greek words *drachma* and *obol,* before coming to refer to coins, signified "handful" and "brooch." Such practices were not very widespread.

More frequent was the use of stamped metal. Impressing a symbol, such as a seal, in the metal does not enable weighing to be dispensed with, but there is no need for a touchstone. Perhaps this was the case in the twenty-second Egyptian dynasty with the silver called "from the treasure of Ptah." In Ur (Mesopotamia) from very early times, and later in Assyria, documents mention silver stamped with the head of Ishtar. The temples seem to have played the vital part in the stamping process.

In all these fumbling attempts, it sometimes happened that a close approach was made to inventing the coin: for example, when the stamp was impressed on a metal piece of exactly one unit of weight (e.g., a shekel) or a simple fraction thereof (third of a *mina*). In reality there would then have been nothing further to invent to have a genuine coin; or rather, nothing further except to be aware of this fact and to maintain the practice over a prolonged period. But the centuries passed, the practice was abandoned, and the coin only appeared in true form much later in history.

B. Money

The coin results from the combination of measurement and stamping. It is in fact defined as a piece of metal of any shape, whose composition and weight is permanently laid down, so that testing and weighing are pointless. When making payments, it is sufficient to count the coins.

1. THE INVENTION OF MONEY

The appearance of the coin is dated at about 700 B.C. Even in antiquity men were already disputing about the place where it was first produced, but the geographical difference between the two viewpoints involved is small: in any case, the area in question lay in western Asia Minor.

According to a hardy tradition expounded by Herodotus,

money was invented by the Lydians, active traders who have been called "the Phoenicians of the Land." Their capital city, Sardis, dominated a river, the Pactolos, which washed down pebbles of electrum, a natural alloy of gold and silver. The last of their kings, Croesus, was believed to be fabulously rich but he was defeated by Cyrus and was fated to suffer a miserable end, about which the Greeks philosophized interminably. After some attempts by his predecessors, Croesus issued, toward the middle of the sixth century B.C., coins called "croeseids," and he established a fixed ratio (1:13 1/3) between silver and gold in the coin. On the basis of this system, he struck some coins of pure gold, some of silver, and also some of electrum; the latter were not very practical because the proportion of silver varies from 20 to 48 per cent in this alloy without appreciable change in color.

According to most present-day numismatists, however, more probably the coin was invented in the Ionian towns of Asia Minor—Ephesos, Miletos, Phocaea (Phokaia). The oldest coins come in the form of lozenges, not circular and flat-sided, but ovoid and convex in the center, bearing on one side an impressed hollow (later on, an embossment) and on the other a simple form of milling ("frill") designed to prevent fraudulent clipping of the metal. We have such coins issued in Ephesos prior to 650 B.C., made of electrum. A little later, the real flat-sided, almost circular coin appeared; the truly circular coin is not earlier than the sixteenth century A.D., with the mint stamp. Until that time, coins were struck by stamping a figurine with a hammer onto the piece, which is placed in a matrix on an anvil; this crushes the metal and forces it to spread slightly beyond the edge of the matrix.

2. THE SPREAD OF MONEY

Money spread rapidly in the Hellenic world along the east-west axis. From Asia Minor, it soon reached European Greece. Around 670, coins were struck in the island of

Aigina. Athens had her own coinage shortly after 600. Gradually, the invention reached Massilia, in the fourth century B.C. Since gold was very scarce, coins were nearly always of silver.

The slowness of the rest of the world is remarkable. In Babylon, the coin did not come into use before the Persian conquest of 539. And it appears that, up to the third century B.C., in spite of the existence of coins, the custom in Babylon of weighing the metal was preserved; this was either to facilitate interchange between pieces of differing weight, or simply as routine. In the Persian Empire, Darius issued (*ca.* 515 B.C.) gold darics which bore the image of the king drawing a bow; and also silver shekels, which were called "Median shekels" to distinguish them from the shekel-weight, since they only weighed just over 5 grams, 1/100 not 1/60 *mina.* Their respective values retained the ratio set by Croesus. This gold coinage gave Darius immense prestige, but was not really designed for anything more than external use —especially with the Greeks: it served for trading, for paying off Greek mercenaries, for bribery (the 30,000 archers who chased the Spartan king Agesilaos out of Asia). But otherwise the tributes paid in specie to the Great King were to rest undisturbed (melted down and cast into jars) in the cellars of the palaces at Susa, Persepolis, or Pasagardae. In Egypt, bronze money spread somewhat, but payment in kind remained in use for a long time, and it was only at a late stage (*ca.* 360 B.C.) that a king of the Thirtieth Dynasty (Takhos) paid off Greek mercenaries by issuing gold pieces having the same weight as darics, but bearing an image of the Athenian owl and her name. The same slowness to adopt coinage can be seen in the non-Hellenic West. It was about 400 B.C. at the earliest that the Carthaginians imitated the Greeks by striking (in Sicily) their first coins, mainly of bronze. The Etruscans and Romans undoubtedly followed them in the course of the fourth century.

3. CONSEQUENCES OF THE INVENTION OF MONEY

From the stage of the metal economy onwards, a real revolution began in economics. Large-scale trade was possible, and the bankers, who were also (and primarily) money changers, played an important part thereafter. In the social order, the appearance of money was soon followed by a crisis, in Athens about 600, later in Rome. This was provoked by interest-loan debts, perhaps because it was impossible for farmers who had borrowed money to repay in metallic coinage rather than by means of the commodities traditionally used.

The appearance of real money also had legal consequences. The first coinages were probably private issues: the earliest Greek coin we have, an Ephesian issue, carries the picture of a stag and the phrase "I am the badge of Phanes," doubtless a banker. But the state intervened very soon to ensure the quality, statutory purity, and weight of metal; it soon reserved the monopoly for itself, making only its own coinage legal currency and legal tender, which thus obliged everyone to accept it as payment at the rate set by the state. From now on, the value-stamp became more important than the commodity bearing it. Money became fiduciary, and was based on the public's confidence—imposed, what is more, from above. Money tended to be self-sufficient, and this opened the door to a new possibility which was exploited almost at once: devaluation. This can be carried out in two ways: one can either reduce the weight per coin but stamp the same value on it; or replace pure metal by an alloy of precious and base metals, using copper or lead as an alloy-additive to silver. Devaluation is an invention scarcely less old than that of money per se. Even Aristotle in the fourth century B.C. felt obliged to say that money was only an accepted convention, a trifle, "a pure nothing."

V. THE ECONOMY IN CLASSICAL GREECE

Between the sixth and fourth centuries B.C., the Greek economy was rocketing. To realize this, it is enough to compare it with the situation in the vast Persian Empire. The unity of this empire and its money were both contributions favorable to the economy. The empire was responsible for great feats of civil engineering: making or renewing the canal between the Nile and the Red Sea, constructing the great "Royal Roads," of which that between Susa and Sardis was the best known because it led toward Greece. It was also in this period that, for the first time, the caravan route of the silk trade (from Persia to China) appeared; and that silk first reached the West. Even all that was still not enough to bring about a high level of prosperity, however. The king thought almost solely of collecting tributes, in kind or in precious metal, and these tributes soon became very heavy; a situation aggravated by the greed of the satraps. Tribute did not help the economy much; it paid for the army, warfare, and the unprecedented luxury of the court, which was supplied regularly with slaves and luxury dogs, and the metal not spent was to remain unused in the cellars of royal palaces. These methods did not succeed in rousing lazy populations, so that when Alexander arrived in Babylon he found canals clogged up and some districts gone to waste.

This apathy is in contrast with the amazing dynamism of the Greeks. In their case, it was trade that carried the whole economy with it. Production had to adjust to it, and great social problems resulted from this.

A. The Rapid Progress of Commerce

Athenian economics gives one an impression somewhat similar to that of Europe in the nineteenth century, making all necessary allowances for the different eras. The difference, considerable of course, is nevertheless quantitative rather than qualitative. Economic life was already most complex. Moreover, it dominated politics and diplomacy. Just the same, a curious discord proved to exist between this reality and public opinion. Although trade expanded, and built the greatness of Athens, the general feeling was traditionalist and distrustful; it contrasted the "economy" founded on agriculture with the "chrematistic" approach, founded on money, to which Aristotle expressed everyone's hostility. This did not hinder any Athenian, who had the chance, from participating in commercial enterprises.

The Athenian legislator showed himself to be very liberal, except in respect of trade in grain, whose cornering and export he forbade. Otherwise he limited himself to ensuring the honesty of business activity by enacting a simple form of commercial law and by controlling weights and measures. In a state so small, customs duty, which was very low, could not lead toward any kind of protectionism.

1. DISTRIBUTION OF COMMODITIES

In a country as mountainous as Greece, land transportation is difficult and expensive. Even between neighboring towns, shipping by sea was the method mainly relied upon. Technological development was still limited, despite the invention of the anchor, in the seventh century B.C. The innumerable harbors were equipped as ports. The largest and a quite recent one, Piraeus, the gateway to Athens, was equipped with piers and roofed colonnades serving as warehouses; a marketplace; and even a stock exchange, where purchases were made on the basis of samples. Very soon this became a world mart.

An important new phenomenon now appeared: besides luxury goods, slaves, and minerals, the traditional items of nonlocal trading, heavy freight began to be shipped. The first wares seem to have been raw materials (hides, wool, timber) and manufactured objects (everyday, not just luxury items). Soon after this came trade in foodstuffs: wine, oil, dried or salted fish, then wheat. Large-scale shipping of wheat came last. Once again one must distinguish between (1) occasional shipments, in time of scarcity or war (e.g., at the time of the wars with the Medes, Syracuse offered to supply the Greeks with food till the end of the campaign); and (2) regular imports. Athens was soon to subsist largely on the corn of Magna Graecia, or of the Pontus Euxinus (what we would call the Ukraine). To pay for these goods, the Greeks exported mainly wine and oil in artistically decorated jars, today the pride of our museums. Athens nevertheless imported more than she exported, and made up the deficit in her trade balance by using silver from her mines as payment.

Although it is true that Grecian trade with the Persian Empire (usually hostile), and with Egypt, was rather inactive, its overall expansion was considerable; and one can begin to describe its economy as, if not worldwide, at least international. Greek did not only trade with Greek wherever colonies were established, but also with Etruscans, Carthaginians, or peoples who were then barbarian (Scythians, Gauls). Archaeological finds mark out the trade routes for goods coming from or entering Greece: the tin route which crossed Gaul (cf. the Vix treasure on the Côte d'Or), and the amber route, as far as the Baltic.

2. CURRENCY

As late as the sixth century B.C., a definite barter economy persisted in Greece. Farm rentals, wages and taxes were paid in kind. Minting of money was hindered by the scarcity of precious metals and by hoarding practiced even by temples, like the extremely rich sanctuary of Apollo at Delphoi. In the fifth century, the discovery of silver mines such as those at Laurion (Laurium) in Attica, and the squandering of treasure during wartime, helped to bring about the spread of monetary economy.

Trade was not, however, assisted by what has been called "the war of the money standards." Each city, even the very small, had its coinage and saw it as a mark of sovereignty. Certain states which were transient and small are only known to historians by the coins discovered there. As a result of this diversity of coinages, the *drachma* varied from 2.90 grams in Corinth to 6.28 in Aigina. There were two chief systems in mutual competition. The heavy *drachma* of Aigina, stamped with the image of a tortoise, spread throughout the Peloponnesus. Athens from Solon's time (594) adopted the Euboic standard (used on the island of Euboia) which was lighter in weight (*ca.* 4.25 grams). The coins were of Laurion silver, stamped with the barn owl, emblem of Athens; were in use over the whole maritime empire of Athens; and were copied as far away as Gaza and Egypt. Their success was due not just to the political success of Athens, but to their probity, since the coins were almost pure silver, of scrupulously checked weight; and Athens never devalued her currency even in wartime.

Some other cities were not so honest. Not only were there constant devaluations, but many small towns when financially embarrassed falsified their currencies and issued "plated" coins, made of copper or lead and clad with a thin silver layer; this device produced some brief and scandalous rewards.

Gold only became widespread in the fourth century. Macedonia had gold mines in Thrace (Mt. Pangaios), and issued coins soon to be named "philips," after her kings. This issue led to a fall in the value of gold relative to silver from 13 1/3:1 to 12:1, and at times to 10:1.

3. MOVEMENT OF CAPITAL

Aristotle, who merely expressed the general view, wrote on the subject of interest loans a sophism which had an extraordinary success in the Middle Ages: the interest loan is to be condemned because interest is a sort of offspring of silver itself; and this is against nature since silver is not reproductive. He was really thinking of loans with a view to consumption, of the petty usury so dangerous to farmers. The production loan, which allows initiation or development of business, does not deserve this severity, and it spread widely in the Greek world. In commercial matters, the rate of interest was then one *drachma* per *mina,* or 1 per cent per month. To this was added compound interest, under the name "anatocism." This "rent" on money was increased still higher, but was an appreciable drop on what it once was in Babylon.

In maritime affairs there was a special loan (later called "bottomry loan") which was a burden on shipping and cargo. In case of shipwreck, the borrower was exempt from the whole debt. But if the ship made it safely to port, interest was due, over and above the capital sum, which could amount to 30 per cent for a seven-month voyage, and even to 100 per cent in wartime. This exorbitant rate of interest, which men justified on the ground of the risks, amounted to a kind of insurance premium.

Solon having established the right to form business partnerships, these became numerous in Athens. They exhibited there what we should call "an ethical personality," which was rare, if not virtually unique, in antiquity. Athens invented, at least for one of the Laurion mines, the form of the joint stock company: many Athenians held one or several shares in this mining company.

A new force appeared in Athens: the bank. Bankers were often foreigners, metics (*metikoi*) or freedmen; furthermore, they were usually looked at askance and Aristotle said: "the profession of handling money is justly hated." They formed small companies, such as the famous Pasion bank, which held an important position in Athenian life around 400 B.C. Besides individuals, certain towns also practiced banking, and sometimes held a monopoly in their territory. The same procedure was used by certain temples (like that of Apollo at Delphoi), which thus increased the value of gifts paid into their treasury.

The bankers were primarily money changers, necessary because of the increasing number of standards of coinage. In addition, they received deposits from their clients and, logically enough, undertook to make payments and debt recoveries for their benefit. A combination of deposit and currency exchange constitutes a letter of credit.[3] For example, an Athenian about to depart on a journey deposits funds with his banker, who sends a letter to one of his colleagues in Miletos; here, the Athenian can obtain on arrival the equivalent in local money of the amount he paid over. Lastly, bankers operated a third procedure: the loan; or, speaking more generally, they participated in various enterprises and became men of wide business interests. Bankers were just as powerful in Asia Minor at the end of the sixth century: one of them, a creditor of Xerxes, was rightly or wrongly believed to have the fabulous sum of 2,000 talents of silver (*ca.* 60 British or 66 American tons), and nearly 4 million gold darics.

The great mobility of capital, continually invested in new enterprises, naturally resulted in speculation. In Athens and elsewhere there existed genuine, small stock exchanges, which differed from ours only in an absence of regulations. During these tumultuous palavers in the Agora or in Piraeus, people were on the watch for all the news, and prices underwent violent fluctuations. Very soon men developed the idea of getting rich by cornering the market: in about 585, the famous mathematician Thales of Miletos, inventor of meteorology, foresaw a good olive crop, bought or rented all the oil presses, and thus made himself a fortune. In wartime, some people bought up all the available iron; others got hold of all the grain in anticipation of the threatened shortages.

B. Effects on Production

In the maritime towns, whatever survived of economic autarchy, provincial or urban, disappeared in the Classical era, and everything was oriented toward buying and selling.

[3] It is not possible as yet to talk of the bill of exchange because this is transferred by means of a promissory note, a much later invention.

These transformations had, all in all, beneficial results for industry and harmful ones for agriculture.

1. IN INDUSTRY

Ferrous metallurgy was quite rare until about 600 B.C. but then became an everyday affair, and certain inventions facilitated this: welding, in Chios, and new smelting processes in Samos. Iron, now cheaper, enabled hoplites to be equipped in large numbers, which led to democratization of the military profession, and this had many political repercussions.

These technological developments, however relatively important, were nevertheless extremely simple. There was no equipment or plant worthy of the name, no machinery, nor motive force other than human. Businesses were on a very small scale: if they had as many as twenty workers they were impressive for those times. A weapons workshop with 120 personnel is cited as a phenomenon. In one mine, one thousand slaves were at work, but in another quite close by, the owner himself went down to the pit-bottom, pick on shoulder, along with a few slaves as workmates. It could happen that one and the same person had several businesses or mines, but not merged or integrated, and this multiplied rather than reduced the overall costs.

The most important transformation concerned markets. Production was aimed at the export, not at the local markets. Greece exported mainly products of her metallurgical and ceramic industries (it is known that the word "ceramic" comes from the name of a district in Athens where potters worked). The disadvantage of this orientation was the frequent occurrence of crises of overproduction and of slumps.

2. IN AGRICULTURE

Agriculture remained very well thought of: "It is the most honored profession because it supplies the city with its finest citizens" (Xenophon). Greece (especially Attica) was, however, the arena of a real revolution in agriculture, because production was aimed at trade instead of at immediate, direct consumption. Pericles astonished his contemporaries greatly the day he sold the harvest from his land and went to buy food in the market; but others followed his example. Thenceforward the growing of grain was neglected, since imports enabled one to buy it cheaper. As early as the fifth century, Attica was no longer self-sufficient in foodstuffs. The area of operations thus vacated was taken over by arboriculture—fruit-trees and above all the vine and the olive—and this was also advised by certain governments such as those of Athens and Syracuse. The substitution had its advantages: wine and oil sold well, and the vines and trees held soil gullied by rainstorms. But in wartime wheat was not able to reach the area; the menace of famine appeared and provoked unrest.

These changes brought with them a great expansion in agriculture. Cultivation became more intensive, and cattle-raising tended to disappear. Land was cleared for tillage, and crop-rotation often replaced fallowing. Treatises on agronomy were written. But in the end, agriculture was to decline. Writers tried to explain this by all kinds of ethical reasoning, but in reality it was the poverty of Greece that emptied her lands once the frontiers were opened. Many Greeks emigrated, often to become mercenaries in the armies of the kings of Persia or Egypt. Soon complaints were raised about the drop in population.

C. Social Consequences

This enormous economic expansion was not universally beneficial, and the history of Greece in the Classical period is marked by serious social problems. These were not just due to economic upheavals but also to political causes: the people fought against the oligarchy of the *Eupatridai,* the great families. It was in Athens that the story is best known, but many other cities underwent analogous crises.

The first crisis occurred in 600 B.C. and was settled by

Solon, archon in 594 (or 592 according to other chronologies). Besides genuinely political quarrels (which Solon was also to settle by a democracy of qualified voters), disagreement resulted from two social phenomena which were perhaps interconnected. There were in Attica many small-scale farmers, the "hektemeroi." The etymology of the word is "one-sixth part": probably these farmers owed the landowners five-sixths of the crop and only kept the one-sixth part.* The land was posted, which signified the ownership of the *Eupatridai,* and the farmers owed their five-sixths to this truly feudal system. The farmers also suffered the scourge of high-interest debts, and when not able to pay were sold into slavery or exiled. Solon freed land by pulling up the boundary markers, which ended the dominion of the *Eupatridai.* To solve the debt problem he issued the *seisachtheia* edict, a term we can translate as "exoneration" (unburdening). We do not know whether to understand by this that debts were abolished, or simply that the interest rate was reduced. All that is certain is that he prohibited slavery for debt; he freed those who had been subjected to it and recalled the exiles. A similar result was obtained indirectly by another of his reforms: a change in the standard of coinage, i.e., substitution of the Euboic *drachma* for the Aigina *drachma.* By this devaluation the debtor, to pay off a debt of the same nominal amount, only needed to hand over a small weight of metal. All these measures procured a long period of social peace for Athens.

In the fifth century, the cities of Greece can be separated into two groups. There were always those dominated by the aristocrats, where landownership reigned supreme. These cities usually sided with Sparta. But the small property owners were mostly in the democratic cities, who looked to Athens then at the height of her greatness. There, most of

* Not all historians agree that five-sixths was paid and one-sixth retained: A. Andrews, Oxford University, states the opposite (cf. Hugh Lloyd-Jones, ed., *The Greek World* [Baltimore: Penguin, 1966], p. 40).—TRANSLATOR'S NOTE.

the landowners had less than six hectares and Aristotle said that no one was destitute at that time, as the land was divided amongst all. Nevertheless, about half the Athenians had no land, but they were not paupers because the Athenian republic subscribed to a policy of social democracy. As a result of various measures, bread was cheap. By means of large-scale undertakings in the field of public works and in the army and navy, the state created employment. Citizens received pay vouchers for attendance at assemblies and tribunals (*misthophoria*). For several years (410–406 B.C.), there was even a small dole paid to paupers. In this way a stable equilibrium was maintained as long as the state was prosperous enough to defray the costs.

Trouble recurred in the fourth century, however, Athens was ruined by the Peloponnesian War and the land was too poor to support the population. Large-scale property ownership was gradually restored by concentration of small pieces of land into the hands of purchasers. Many of the poor emigrated and depopulation ensued, the *oliganthropia* discussed by the moralists. Whereas in the Periclean era Athens had over 40,000 citizens, excluding aliens, by 315 she had no more than 21,000, despite many naturalizations. Furthermore, the social situation was aggravated by the brazen luxury displayed by the rich. The poor demanded land distribution and, once more, abolition of debts. The democratic party then enacted measures typical of the demagogue: in Athens, after giving the poor relief pay for food, they issued more for theatergoing. The aristocrats later took over the reins, and then abolished the civil rights of the poor along with these relief payments. This led to civil war. With a total lack of patriotism, each side when in danger appealed to foreign nations. There were dreadful massacres. The orator Isocrates wrote: "Those in possession would sooner have flung their property into the sea than have assisted the poor, and the poorest derived less satisfaction from seizing the wealth of the rich than from the act of depriving them of it."

It was also said in Syracuse, about the middle of the fourth century: "For the unfortunate, equality is the beginning of liberty; poverty, of servitude." No remedy was ever found for this situation. The ideal state proposed by Plato, where one sometimes sees a remote forerunner of communist theories, was never taken seriously; and besides, his communism, if the name is deserved, was a communism of aristocracy. The aristocrats and democrats succeeded each other in power alternately, without in the least solving the problem, for three centuries until the Roman conquest.

CHAPTER TWO

The Hellenistic Era

"Hellenistic," as opposed to "Hellenic," is the term for the world and civilization of Grecian type established by the victories of Alexander, and its unity was maintained despite rapid political partition. The battle of Actium in 31 B.C., along with the disappearance of the last kingdom resulting from these victories, marks the end of the period, although the Roman Empire inherited this civilization. From the viewpoint of economics, the Hellenistic world was a very important and advanced region, on the edge of which Carthage lagged behind until her collapse: she will be examined in the first section of the chapter.

I. THE HELLENISTIC AND CARTHAGINIAN WORLD

In this relatively extensive geographical grouping (stretching all the way from Mesopotamia to Gibraltar) the general conditions exhibit certain common features, but some countries evolved in an individual way or preserved a particular pattern of behavior; such were Greece, Egypt, and Carthage.

A. The General Conditions of Hellenistic Economics

From the Greek viewpoint, this era was only the sequel of the preceding one, with purely quantitative changes. Yet the

Greeks found many new things in the former Persian Empire: a vast area, with regions like Egypt and Mesopotamia endowed with great resources; a large, obedient but apathetic population; absolute monarchy, which allowed state planning. Lastly, they found huge gold and silver reserves, valued at 180,000 talents and until then stored in the palaces, and which were immediately squandered; this gave an impetus to economics comparable with that in sixteenth-century Europe, when flooded with specie in the wake of the discovery of Eldorado.

To this conquered land the Greeks brought, first of all, their dynamic approach, their spirit of enterprise and initiative; then, their commercial and banking methods and the plentiful circulation of money. Considerable traffic in goods and even foodstuffs was to take place in these areas, often for the first time. Lastly, the Greeks brought their urban economy, and founded many cities: all the Alexandrias, of which the most famous was in Egypt, besides those named Ptolemais, Berenice, Arsinöe, Philadelphia, and in Seleukid country, Seleukia, Laodikeia, Apameia, twenty-four called Antiocheia (Antioch) and others whose name perpetuated the memory of kings or queens. All in all, there were many changes.

1. THE EXPANSION IN PRODUCTION

In this, to them, new country, the Greeks discovered new resources and an extreme diversity of land: very rich areas under intensive cultivation, such as Egypt, Mesopotamia, Coele-Syria; the coastal plains of Asia Minor; and vast steppelands traversed by the herds of nomads. They learned to grow palm trees, Egyptian oil seeds, papyrus, the lotus, even to some extent cotton and sorghum. On their side, they introduced the vine or greatly extended its growth, for it was almost unknown in Egypt and Mesopotamia. They also discovered minerals such as saltpeter, used for laundering, the Dead Sea asphalt, the liquid naphtha of Assyria (which is actually petroleum oil)—of which Strabo wrote that people there had the strange idea of using it like oil in lamps. They also obtained innumerable mineral beds and learned new methods of ore extraction, as for rock salt of the lakes and mountains of Asia Minor.

So far as manual labor was concerned, slavery was on the wane until the time when, by their slave-buying, the Romans were to incite the pirates (the suppliers) to obtain men by every possible means. Nevertheless slavery was very important, specially in the Seleukid kingdom: the great royal domains were cultivated by slaves, who owned their own cattle and sometimes their houses, but had to pay rent; they were tied to the land, and were conveyed with it in transactions. Above all there existed a plentiful supply of labor, legally free but subject to the corvée; not to mention the (de facto at least) hereditary nature of professions; this labor was very cheap. Greeks and Macedonians, for their part, became immigrants. Most became officials or soldiers, but these soldiers were settlers ("cleruchs"); they paid rent and served in the army. Such tenancies were very widespread in Egypt and evolved gradually toward private ownership.

Among the various enterprises, of widely differing magnitude, we see large undertakings belonging to owners by right of state law: kings, autonomous towns, and temples. First, there were the vast estates such as the "royal lands" of Egypt, farmed by "royal cultivation"; the 4,500 hectares of the Temple of Horus at Edfu; in Asia Minor, the estates of Cybelle at Pessinonte or of Ma (Bellona) at Comana, whose cultivation was ensured by the hierodules, slaves sacred to the goddess, amounting to as many as 6,000 on a single estate. There were also mines, quarries, and salt pans; workshops for embroidery, luxury fabrics and ceramics; the royal stud farms of Apameia in Syria, maintaining a permanent stock of 30,000 brood mares and 500 elephants.

The Greeks carried out large-scale public works, or had them carried out by others; repair of dikes, dredging of silted canals, in Egypt and Mesopotamia. Under Ptolemy II Philadelphus, they had vast areas drained in El Fayum around

Lake Moeris. They sometimes introduced new techniques: the system of two crops per year seems to have been imposed in Egypt by the same Ptolemy. Technological inventions were put into practice such as the suction and piston pumps, the water mill, otherwise little used, or the worm screw and a hydraulic machine, due to the genius of Archimedes.

2. THE EXPANSION IN COMMERCE

In the Hellenistic era, commerce was more important than ever, and extended further afield. Its methods were always those of the Greeks, including speculation, and cornering the market, the most famous since the beginning of the period being the exploit of the governor of Egypt, Kleomenes, appointed by Alexander: he banned all exports of wheat from the country, bought up the whole harvest, and by means of suitably spaced shipments to Greece (then suffering a shortage) made a huge profit.

a. Transportation and Trade Routes. Cabotage always involves the watchtower and a new version was invented—the lighthouse, whose name is derived from that famous structure built on the island of Pharos at the entrance to Alexandria harbor.

The main trade routes converged on the Aegean Sea or on Seleukia, the new Seleukid capital on the Tigris. Alexandria was the starting point of those southerly routes leading to the Red Sea, whether up the Nile and via the bend at Koptos, or along the canal through the Suez isthmus, put into operation again by Ptolemy Philadelphus. Navigation extended as far as East Africa, Arabia, and India. This was the first time the corn of Egypt reached India, and a new Sanskrit word was coined for it: *alisandaga,* the produce of Alexandria. The Greek Hippalos discovered the phenomenon of the periodic monsoon, which made it possible to sail to India and return by it.

To travel east, traders went to the great bend of the Euphrates either via Antiocheia (Antioch) or, starting from Ephesos, by a long road which crossed Asia Minor. They then traveled down the Euphrates or along it as far as Seleukia, whence roads or trails radiated outwards toward the Persian Gulf and India, or toward Persia and Bactriana (Turkestan), in the direction of China. Traveling northeast, the Greeks always went towards the Pontus Euxinus, whence roads or riverways led them to the Caspian Sea. In a westerly direction (*ca.* 320 B.C.) the Massiliot Pytheas journeyed to the mysterious island of Thule—perhaps to the north of Great Britain, or in Norway.

Two large transit depots grew up in the Aegean. First, Rhodes, center of Greek trade with Egypt, through which the grain was routed. It is famous in history for its maritime laws which the Romans later adopted. But it declined from the middle of the second century in favour of Delos, where the Romans set up a free port in 166 B.C. Delos became the largest slave market supplying Italy, owing to raids carried out by Cilician pirates, who finally destroyed it in 69 B.C.

b. Money. Because the Greeks had squandered the treasures of the Persian kings, money was now far more plentiful than before. It spread not only amongst the Greeks but all through the Orient, despite some persistence of barter economics in Babylon and Egypt. There were gold pieces in existence, but silver was the leading currency: for example, in Egypt, silver pieces remained constant while the weight of other coins changed to follow the variations in value-ratio of gold to silver. Bronze and copper were just change-money except in Egypt, where the Ptolemies, in order to reserve silver for foreign trade, tried to make bronze specie the national money for domestic use; and they issued pieces of about 90 grams, the metal in the coin being worth about the same as its nominal value. Inflation soon ruined the attempt.

Among the various monetary standards which persisted—there was no monetary unity in the Hellenistic world—three types emerged. The Athenian *drachma* adopted by Alexander for his whole empire was only retained by the Seleukids. It weighed *ca.* 4.25 grams. Rhodes had a lighter *drachma, ca.* 3.25 grams, which became adopted throughout Asia Minor. Egypt hesitated between the two precedents and finally adopted an intermediate standard, *ca.* 3.55 grams.

Naturally, there were many devaluations. Inflation became serious in Egypt after 234 B.C., and she never succeeded in curing it before the end of her period of independence.

c. The Bank. Among the various banking operations, many payments seem to have been made [1] without transfer of solid coin, thanks to devices resembling our checks and clearinghouses. Money based on the note of hand * therefore dates back to antiquity.

The bankers included private individuals, temples who turned their treasure to account, cities and states. The greatest power in the banking world was the Royal Bank of Egypt, granted a wide monopoly. Its headquarters were in Alexandria, but it had branches in the smallest towns or country villages. It was duplicated in the case of wheat by a parallel network of public granaries, actually general stores, which were likewise established in all small market towns or villages. Payments in wheat were also made simply by accounting, without transfer of the actual commodity. This double series of banks (in money and wheat) played a leading part in the economy. The officials and small craftsmen had bank accounts, which gave the state an extremely effective means of control, because it could freeze the accounts at any time. This royal bank also made loans, but had no monopoly here.

B. The Decline of Greece

Against this background, certain countries were conspicuous for their individual forms of development. For mainland

[1] Cf. F. Preisigke, *Girowesen,* 1910, which has been subject to criticism, however.

* Lévy's term is *monnaie scripturale,* i.e., all forms of true money not involving banknotes or specie, such as bills of exchange, bank accounts, etc. —Translator's Note.

and island Greece this period, so brilliant in other ways, was one of decline, which had already begun before Alexander, and which continued to worsen. The basic reason was competition from new countries; it did not so much affect trade as production, and resulted in shocks to the social system.

Agrarian poverty spread. Deprived of seed and up to the ears in debt, the peasants sold off their land. The big landowners thereby benefited so as to reform their holdings, but the large estates were poorly cultivated and often went back to pasturage, even to heath or brush. Two-thirds of the island of Euboia, once very fertile, was left to run wild, as were certain areas of Thessaly.

Some remarkable products of this period, such as the famous statuettes of Tanagra (a small town in Boiotia), should not lead one to forget the general decline of industry. Many enterprises, such as the Laurion silver mines during much of the third century and the naval dockyards in Piraeus, were held up for lack of timber. Unemployment is significant from the outset of the third century. Wages fell faster than the cost of living and then stagnated when living costs began to rise in the middle of the third century. Pay at pre-agreed rates became general, and was combined with auctioning at rock-bottom pay for men's labor: for fear of unemployment, artisans preferred to work for low pay rather than risk the danger.

This state of affairs had certain social consequences. People in those days complained of depopulation (*oliganthropia*). It is a fact that many daughters were "exposed" (abandoned at birth). As soon as they reached adulthood, many men emigrated and became soldiers or cleruchs overseas. On the other hand, social conflict persisted, from strikes to civil war. The traditional demands for land distribution and abolition of debts took on a particularly violent tone. The demands were in fact met. Certain towns in Thessaly bought land and distributed it to the poor but the experiment failed. In Sparta (241 B.C.), King Agis abolished debts but was forthwith murdered.* The oligarchs appealed for help to Macedonia, then Rome. But this decline in the realm of practical affairs did not reduce the intellectual brilliance of Greece, especially of Athens, which continued to be the mother-city of the civilized world.

C. The Egyptian State-controlled Economy [2]

Within the Hellenistic world, Egypt kept some individual features of her own. Firstly, her economic power: she was the wheat granary of the East. The revenue of her kings far exceeded those of the others. Her population, estimated at seven million, was large for this period. On the other hand, state control of, or interference in, the economy was far more extensive than elsewhere. It was an old tradition of the country but it reached its peak at this period, doubtless because of the superposition of one social stratum on another: the extremely passive native subjects were under the very dynamic Greeks, who exploited them to the limit.

State control and intervention can lead to different goals, and nothing shows this better than a comparison between the pharaohs and the Ptolemies in this respect. The state socialism of the latter had absolutely no social aims, only mercantile and fiscal ones. It was all a matter of filling the king's coffers, and providing him with resources devoted to a policy of glory and conquest in the Hellenistic world.

1. The Methods

There was a real omnipresence of the state under the Lagid rulers. It operated by a network of different empirical techniques which kept control of the producers from all sides; producers ordinarily provided nothing but their labor, yet remained responsible for the results of the productive process.

The first method was that of state capitalism, i.e., the state

* Judicially, not by the intended beneficiaries.—Translator's Note.

[2] C. Préaux, *L'économie royale des Lagides* (Brussels, 1939).

owned most of the means of production and exchange and also a large part of the land, quite apart from the fact that it administered the vast estates of the temples, to which it allotted only a budget for religious activities; it owned much livestock; and many enterprises, such as mines, quarries, salt pans, workshops, and fisheries. The state also owned certain work tools, more particularly iron ones, which it lent or rented to workers. Another method of control was the loan, in money or seed. The state had the monopoly of the seeds of oleaginous grain, and the farmers were forced to "borrow" it from the state. Interest rates were very high: 24 per cent per annum for money loans, 50 per cent for seed; and payments were due in six months. We must remember also the double, parallel network of the Royal Bank (money and granaries), through which passed the vast majority of payments, all under state control.

The state likewise intervened by employing widely all its public law prerogatives. Even though it seldom requisitioned goods or persons, it reserved for itself innumerable monopolies in purchase, sale, and warehousing. The most absolute was that of oil. Oil-grain seeds (sesame, croton, castor oil) were always loaned to the cultivator at interest. The whole harvest was sold to farmers of the state monopoly and producers did not even have the right to keep grain with a view to the next campaign. It was the administration alone which supplied the retailers, and all prices were fixed by fiat at all levels. To appropriations due as interest on loans, there were added those taken as taxes paid in kind. Finally, the protectionist customs-dues kept Egypt isolated: they rose to 33 per cent, even to 50 per cent (while in other countries they rarely exceeded 2 or 5 per cent).

Control took on frightening proportions. There was a whole army of inspectors. There were nothing but inventories, censuses of men and animals, land surveys, estimations of harvests to come. Harvests, once gathered, were guarded by armed peasants. Unoccupied workshops, and tools momentarily unused, were sequestered. Goods and payments were frozen in the granaries and banks until the state had taken its share.

This whole network was completed by a system of joint responsibilities. In villages, when farmers who were disgusted with all these vexations ran away, those who remained were responsible for absentees' production, and the abandoned land was officially redistributed amongst them. The officials were likewise responsible: the amounts assessed in advance had to be met, come what might, on pain of being forced to make up the deficit at their own expense. Obviously, they made up their losses from those subject to them; and the pressure they applied extended, in case of need, to cruelty or torture.

2. THE RESULTS

The king derived from all this an unrivaled power. In internal affairs, holding all the keys to the economy, he could plan the whole production and set programs which the responsible officials used their resourcefulness to complete. In external affairs, Alexandria exported far more than she imported, which brought in net receipts of gold and silver: this precocious application of mercantilism drew fabulous royal revenues. Ptolemy II Philadelphus banked about 15,000 talents per annum, and left a considerable treasure after his death. He and his successors could lead lives of great luxury and pomp, and could undertake vast conquests.

But the indigenous laborers suffered from the abuses of state intervention in the economy, and from the "bronze law." * Most people were poor. They had no capital: neither land nor iron tools (a state monopoly), and little livestock. The workers did not own the raw materials they worked up, especially in the case of oil. Oil dealers were only stocked for five days at a time. Farmers had to borrow seed. Fishermen

* *Loi d'airain,* a Malthusian type of economic theory predicting that wages can never exceed a bare minimum for supporting life.—TRANSLATOR'S NOTE.

had to borrow the wherewithal to buy nets. The people no longer had any initiative and endured constraints, administrative pressure, irritating inspections, and beatings. While they did not have the advantages of free enterprise, neither could they be like the carefree wage earner, since they were responsible for the work and took all risks. This inhuman regime led to an attitude of dull endurance in the population.

For the country as a whole, state-run economics brought certain benefits; there was an increase in the area of arable land. One part of El Fayum was drained afresh. New products were introduced. But this progress hardly profited anyone beyond the king and the Graeco-Macedonian colonizers. The drained lands in El Fayum were distributed to the cleruchs—Greek or Macedonian farmer-soldiers. Wool was only bought by the Greeks in Egypt or exported to Greece. Imports were only made for the profit of Greeks. The native inhabitants lived in economic autarchy.

The regime also had its bad side. Egypt was kept out of the world's trade and lived in a closed circuit of its own. Oil was more expensive there than elsewhere; wheat was cheaper, labor costs were less. Her place in the economic evolution is ambiguous: in advance of other lands by virtue of her banking and clearinghouses, she was lagging in monetary matters, because bronze coin and even a degree of barter economy persisted in the interior. After a period of brilliance, Egyptian economy collapsed at the end of the third century B.C., as did her political stability. The financial crisis was a permanency. Money was devalued. Alexandria's commerce declined. Workers, disgusted by the conditions imposed on them, left their lands and disappeared into the country (*anachoresis*), and the sand began to cover once more some of the villages of El Fayum.

D. Carthaginian Isolation

Carthage—the "new town"—was a Tyrian colony founded in 814 B.C. She became independent when her mother city,

Tyre, was destroyed by Alexander in 332 B.C., and she followed the same path as the other Phoenician colonies of the West. The unusual nature of her economy lay mainly in the fact that it lagged behind the general level of economic evolution: it was oriented toward trade with the barbarians, white or Negro, and the Carthaginians turned their backs on their enemies, the Greeks.

1. COMMERCE

Trade dominated both the economy and the whole political situation in Carthage. It was primarily a commerce of transit, based on foreign products with a destination abroad. Carthage reigned in the Mediterranean from the Syrtis Major to the Pillars of Melkarth, and the beginning of the Atlantic coastline. She dominated North Africa; Spain as far as the area around the mouth of the Ebro; Sardinia; and the western third of Sicily, plus Palermo. She held a monopoly of trade and defended it by all means at her disposal. First, by secrecy: there is the well-known story of the Carthaginian ship pursued by a Greek vessel hoping to see her take an unknown * route, but she preferred to run aground on the reefs rather than reveal the passage she was taking. Carthage also defended this monopoly by diplomacy: she signed trade agreements with various powers, notably (according to Polybios) with Rome, in about 509 B.C. perhaps, and certainly in 348 and 280 B.C. While accepting a few Roman vessels in some of her ports, Carthage prohibited them in a certain number of areas. Finally, she defended her monopoly by war, principally against the Greeks. As allies of the Etruscans, Carthaginians temporarily occupied Corsica after the battle of Alalia (535 B.C.). They were defeated by the Syracusans at Himera (480 B.C.), but nevertheless managed to retain a position in part of Sicily. They finally came into conflict with the Romans, which proved to be their downfall. The first

* Unknown to the Greeks.—TRANSLATOR'S NOTE.

Punic War (264 B.C.) was started over the question of Sicily, the second (218 B.C.) over the possession of Saguntum in Spain.

But her commercial methods seem to have been diverted more toward small profits dishonestly acquired than to progress in commercial techniques, and it was probably not unfair of the Romans to ridicule "Punic bad faith." The Carthaginians made a handsome profit by buying at low cost certain luxury items from the barbarians, who were dazzled by their trumpery wares. They shamelessly practiced smuggling and raiding: in the trade agreements with Rome, they promised to abstain—to a certain extent! By contrast, they seem to have lagged behind in regard to the most advanced systems. They knew nothing about running business companies, about banks, or about credit. They probably had no genuine money before 400 B.C. Their first coins were struck in Sicily (copies of the Greek) and then elsewhere. Their coins were quite ugly and did not spread far afield; archaeologists have discovered none beyond the area which was truly Carthaginian. They did have some silver coins (thanks to the mines of Spain) and some gold (to pay off their mercenaries) but generally they used only bronze coins.

2. PRODUCTION

Their industrial production was mediocre. They built ships, made jewelry, glassware, and pottery: the articles were mostly utilitarian, sometimes vulgar, shoddy goods. Their products were lacking in originality: they first copied Egyptian models, then those of Sicilian Greeks. On the other hand, in the territory around Carthage (the half which is north of present-day Tunisia) their agriculture was fairly prosperous, as was their apiculture and raising of the famous Numidian horses. They had several agronomists of note, cited by the Greeks and Romans; in particular one named Mago, author of a treatise in twenty-eight books, which Scipio Aemilianus succeeded in rescuing from the conflagration when he captured Carthage. The Roman Senate had the work translated into Latin. Cicero mentioned it and drew inspiration from it for his *Georgics*. Carthaginian agricultural production was not aimed at exportation, however, and did not always suffice for internal consumption. Africa did not become one of the wheat granaries of Rome until after the Roman conquest.

All in all, the Carthaginians could nonetheless be satisfied with their prosperity, which preserved them after the disasters that befell. Even after the battle of Zama (191 B.C.), they could offer the Romans, at war with the Seleukids, final payment of the imposed war indemnity, without waiting for the anticipated due dates. They also offered to supply ships and grain, gratis. The Romans were suspicious and refused. In the second century they struck some coins in gold, which the Romans were no longer making. They thus aroused the jealousy of Rome and provoked the final catastrophe of 146 B.C.

II. ROMAN PENETRATION INTO THE HELLENISTIC ECONOMY

Italy (except Magna Graecia) had lived apart from the economic and cultural worlds of the Hellenes. Her evolution was very backward. Yet at the beginning of the third century (the Tarentine war), Rome is seen conducting an attack on Magna Graecia. After her decisive victory over Carthage at the beginning of the second century B.C., she defeated first Macedonia and then the Seleukid Empire. The same year (146 B.C.) was marked by the destruction of Carthage and the conquest of Greece. From then on, she dominated the Hellenistic world, not only militarily but economically. After we have examined the economic lag of Rome and Italy in section 1, we shall see how the Romans made up for this delay and succeeded in fitting in to the Hellenistic economy (section 2), so as to exploit their victory to the profit of certain Romans (section 3) but in the end to the detriment of Italy, convulsed by social crises (section 4).

A. The Economic Antecedents in Italy up to the Third Century B.C.

Roman history begins officially in 754 B.C. But the early centuries are far more a matter of legend than of true history. So far as our knowledge goes, we can dimly see the economy of this primitive period as a most unsophisticated one. However, a dynamic element was at work in it—the Etruscans. Their zenith seems to correspond to a transient brilliance in the economy, to be extinguished with their recession. It was not until the end of the period that the Romans achieved a monetary economy, but they were already undergoing social upheavals.

1. The Early Economy of Italy

Before the Etruscan conquest was extended as far as Rome —the legendary date 616 B.C., marked by the coronation of Tarquinius, will serve as a landmark—Roman and Italian economics was both backward and predominantly agrarian. In fact, pastoral economy was the chief feature: the early wars of the Romans against their neighbors the Sabines or Albans were, according to historians, occasioned by the problems of rights of pasturage and of passage for transhumance of animals. Their very primitive type of cultivation, fallowing one year in two, produced grain, beans, and some vegetables, fruits, and a few vines. Pasture lands were probably owned collectively by the patrician *gentes,* while cultivation was a family enterprise, involving the *pater familias,* his wife and children, and perhaps some slaves.

By the middle of the second millennium, Italy was acquainted with copper. Then, in the Terramara period, named after the *terramare* (houses built on piles in the solid earth), invaders, probably from the north, initiated the Bronze Age in Italy. Then came the first Iron Age or "Villanovan" civilization (from the archaeological site at Villanova, near Bologna); it was contemporary with the Dorian invasion of Greece. This introduction of iron into Italy and many other regions is attributed to Indo-European peoples. All this occurred well before the foundation of Rome. According to historians in antiquity, Romulus took from the Etruscans the salt pans at the mouth of the Tiber. His successor, Numa, is supposed to have instituted nine craftsmen's guilds in Rome. That is all we can observe of Italy's primitive industry.

Trade was on a minor scale. This period can be described as one of closed domestic economy, the family unit living independently without external barter. But one must not overstress this characteristic: small-scale exchange always takes place among farmers. Even in Rome, markets were held dating certainly from very ancient times; these were called *nundinae,* since they were held once in every nine days. The pontiffs are also supposed to have constructed in very ancient times a wooden bridge, the *pons Sublicius,* which abutted on the *Forum boarium,* the cattle market. All this indicates at least a rudimentary transportation system. Legend would also have it that Numa concluded agreements with all the neighboring peoples, granting them the right to trade with Rome, and that the fourth king, Ancus Martius, founded the port of Ostia at the mouth of the Tiber: but the first story is uncertain, and no one believes the second.

2. THE ETRUSCAN HEGEMONY

In the seventh and sixth centuries B.C., the Etruscans dominated Italy from the Alps to Capua, and three kings of Rome were Etruscans. The economy developed in all its aspects.

Agriculture benefited from large-scale drainage works. It was the Etruscans who drained the Pontine marshes south of

Rome, and in Rome itself drained the site of the Forum; to remove the water they built the first artificial conduit, the *Cloaca Maxima.* They also drained another marsh in Tuscany itself, the Maremma, and dug channels in the plain of the river Po, opening up vast areas everywhere for cultivation. Tarquin the Elder is alleged to have introduced the olive tree to Rome from Magna Graecia.

Etruscan industry developed in various geographical areas. Their metallurgy was centered on the Tuscany region, where important beds of copper, iron, lead, and silver ores were located; the toponymy here still bears witness today to these beds (e.g., Monte-Argentaro, Piombino, and Porto-Ferrajo on the Isle of Elba). The manufacture of weapons was in full swing at Arretium. In Latium they introduced the manufacture of delicate wares, mirrors and jewels, at Praeneste. In Rome the *Vicus Tuscus,* the Etruscan street or quarter south of the Forum, was enlivened by craft guilds, especially in metalworking. Etruscans were also capable potters, whose famous black-lacquered vases called "bucchero" gave rise to a considerable export trade. Lastly, they were great builders: it was they who built Rome, with her temples and houses of cement, and probably also the wall named after Servius Tullius, unless he lived much later, as certain historians believe.

Despite the absence of money, the Etruscans carried on trade, sometimes in the form of piracy—at least, according to the Greeks, their competitors. They laid out roads, of which two crossed Latium from their own region toward Campania, one passing through Rome. They dominated the Mare Tyrrhenum, thanks to their alliance with Carthage and despite the efforts of the Greeks to bottle them up in the Cumae-Massilia vice. They were large-scale slave traders. They also exported raw materials and some foodstuffs. They imported artifacts from Corinth and Athens. These exchanges are, basically, typical of young countries. They also acted as intermediaries between barbarians and civilized peoples, such as the Greeks of Italy or the Carthaginians. They sold to the

Greeks the amber they had obtained by some unknown means from the shores of the Baltic.

According to Cicero and Titus Livius (Livy), the site of Rome was predestined. Her beginnings were modest, however, as against the whole background of Etruscan economy. She was able, certainly, to set up a market on the drained site of the Forum, and the bridge over the Tiber formed an intersection point for roads. Servius Tullius is supposed to have set up stores on the Forum: they marked the appearance of a sedentary trade, carried out by specialists. He and his successor. Tarquinius Superbus, are said to have granted by treaty the right of Latin peoples to trade with Rome; historians are less doubtful about this than about attributing these same treaties, according to another version, to Numa.

3. THE ROMAN ECONOMY AFTER THE ETRUSCAN REGRESSION

After the Etruscan kings had been expelled from Rome (traditionally 510 B.C.), the Etruscan people continued to decline during the fifth and fourth centuries, probably under the pressure of the Cisalpine Gauls. In 474 B.C., Etruscans and Carthaginians were defeated disastrously off Cumae by the Syracusans. Little by little the Romans encroached into Etruria and subjugated it at the beginning of the third century.

This decline was accompanied by an economic recession lasting about 150 years down to the middle of the fourth century. This period in the internal history of Rome is one of dominance by the patrician element and their *gentes,* regarded by historians as cattle raisers. Pastoral economy outweighed cultivation, and agricultural production was inadequate; this led to famine followed by epidemics, for which the wars were probably not solely responsible. To remedy this, sometimes the state and sometimes the demagogues imported wheat from Etruria, Campania, and Sicily. Commerce was likewise affected: the Etruscan recession closed the doors to the outside world and brought about a degree of dissociation at least from the Hellenic economy, if not from the world economy. It is true that Polybios reports a trade treaty concluded between Rome and Carthage in 509, but many historians have suspected him of being the victim of a confusion of dates.

From the middle of the fourth century, however, and paralleled by her military expansion, Rome's economy began to gain new impetus. She founded colonies on land seized from conquered peoples: not a new institution, but one that began to assume importance at that time. These colonies (Latin: *colere,* to cultivate), peopled by army veterans, were the answer to both strategic and food supply problems at the same time, because they were settlements for Romans or their allies in newly acquired lands. Ostia was colonized at the latest by 350 B.C. For her part, Rome facilitated the circulation of merchandise by the construction of ports and roads. Initially roads were for military purposes only. The oldest, the Via Latina, inherited from the Etruscans, enabled Capua to be reached by an inland route along the foot of the hills. It was duplicated in 312 B.C. by the Via Appia, nearer the coast. In the end, these roads were used for trade. A commercial treaty was concluded in 348 B.C. with Carthage (the historicity of this one is unquestioned) and was followed by several others in 280 B.C. They forbade the Romans access to the African coasts, except at Carthage itself, but allowed them to land at Sardinia and Sicily and to trade there under Carthaginian magistrate control. Other trade treaties were concluded, at the end of the fourth century, with Tarentum and probably with Rhodes, proving the Romans were already traveling far afield. All this colonial and commercial expansion developed increasingly from the third century onward.

4. THE APPEARANCE OF MONEY IN ITALY

The monetary history of Italy and Rome went through the same stages as it did in Greece and the East, but with a very clear-cut time lag relative to those areas. Magna Graecia aside, money appeared late in Italy. The Ligurians have left behind them no money whatever. Neither have the Cisalpine Gauls; they were supposed to have a love for gold, but they handled it on the basis of weight. As in the East, the story can be divided into two stages—the premonetary, and the true monetary.

a. The Premonetary Stage. Almost certainly the Romans used animals as money. *Pecunia* (money) is derived from *pecus,* a small animal. Several laws of 454, 452, and 430 B.C., enacting fines, equate one ox to ten sheep or one hundred *as;* they were certainly drafted or modified in the period when the metal coin *as* had been introduced, and these equivalences permitted passage from the ancient animal money to the new metallic form.

They also employed a technique of using weighed metal. We know that the Gauls, having captured Rome in 390 B.C., had demanded as the price of withdrawal a large amount of gold and that their chief, the famous Brennus, threw his sword into the balance shouting: *"Vae victis."* This story shows that gold went by weight and was not yet specie in Italy.

The Romans also used the *aes rude* (bronze in the lump) by weight. In the formulation of certain legal proceedings (mancipation, *nexum*) which had continued in force for centuries, sometimes well into our era, there occurred the weighing of a piece of bronze, eventually purely symbolic; the ceremony dated back to the times when ingot bronze served as payment money.

The unit of weight was the pound (*libra*) but there were two kinds: the "Roman" pound was 327 grams (1/100 *kikkar,* the Babylonian talent); but to weigh money, a pound called the "Oscan" or "Latin" was used, equivalent to 273 grams or 4/5 of the "Roman." The pound was divided into twelve ounces (*unciae*).

Tradition attributes to the sixth king, Servius Tullius, the invention of stamped metal, the *aes signatum.* This was a bronze ingot provided with a mark guaranteeing its composition. It is true that stamped bronze bricks have been found, but there is nothing to prove that they date back to so ancient a period.

In addition to these various procedures—analogues of those which preceded coinage in Greece and the East—Italy was able to profit by her slowness and employ yet another technique: the use of foreign money, obviously Greek and especially that of Neapolis, of Tarentum, and of all Magna Graecia. The Cisalpine Gauls finally adopted the Massiliot *drachma*. Italy thus went over to a monetary economy before a national coinage existed.

b. The Monetary Stage. National money did appear, but late. It was not until near the end of the fourth century that the Etruscans had any coins, especially copper, some gold (to pay Gallic mercenaries), and also silver, toward the end of their period of independence. The figures on the coins were crudely drawn and were imitations of the Greek.

The oldest Roman coin was the *as*, a term approximating to *aes* (bronze), and in fact it was bronze. It weighed 273 grams, a Latin pound (*as libralis*), and brought with it a smaller coin (1/12 *as*), the *uncia*. But the date of its appearance is highly controversial; the experts hover between the two extremes of 467 and 289 B.C., with many intermediate dates. The most probable date is toward the end of the fourth century, which means that the Romans were nearly four hundred years behind the Greeks.

5. THE FIRST ROMAN SOCIAL CRISIS

The political crisis in which the plebeians opposed the patricians in the fifth and fourth centuries B.C. was paralleled by a social crisis, perhaps the basic cause of the political one. The social upheaval itself certainly resulted from a whole group of circumstances. First of all, the incessant wars of this period: the farmer, when drafted, had to equip himself at his own expense before leaving for battle. If he returned, he found his land gone to waste, sometimes ravaged by the enemy, and his herds slaughtered. He had no seed nor any means of subsistence till the next harvest. The city dwellers must have been ruined by the city fire which the Gauls started in 390. On the other hand, the patricians seem to have constituted a group of pastoral *gentes,* and all herdsmen tend to acquire a monopoly of land for their herds. Perhaps, also, the land taken by conquest from the enemy was acquired by the well-to-do, rather than being equally distributed amongst everyone. Finally, as in the Greece of Solon's time, the appearance of metallic money must have created many difficulties for the farmer. We should add that, at the end of the period, Italy began to abandon the growing of grain and vegetables, which was all to the benefit of arboriculture (vines, olive trees); from then on, it became impossible to live directly off the products of Italian soil. Italy then depended on export, but the market was unstable. This crisis assumed two aspects: agrarian landownership and debts.

a. Agrarian Measures. In 456, the Aventine Hill was apportioned off amongst the plebeians. In 440, there were some legal proposals aimed at the allotment of conquered land, and more than once such proposals were adopted. Colonizations were based on the same idea.

One particular law of this period is famous because it was to be constantly recalled in later times: the *lex Licinia Sextia* (the Licinian law, for short) of 367 B.C. It was supposed to have forbidden possession of a surface area greater than 500 *jugera* per head (*ca.* 126 hectares per person); * the law also is alleged to have divided surplus land amongst the plebeians at two *jugera* per head. It is supposed to have been renewed in 297. But the date 367 and the very existence of a law of this description have both been disputed: certain historians question whether much later measures might not have been pre-dated to cloak them with greater prestige.

* One hectare equals about 2.5 acres.—TRANSLATOR'S NOTE.

b. Measures Taken against Debt. This period was one of sluggish economics and was also primarily agrarian; loans were what economists classify as "expense loans," simply designed to allow the borrower to pay living costs and debts (dues, farm rent, taxes), but not to develop business. At the time when repayment falls due, the borrower is as poor as he was when the loan was granted, so that he has great difficulty in repaying. Furthermore, the agreed interest rates were overwhelming. Lastly, Roman law was very hard on debtors, who were answerable for their debts with their bodies: in case of insolvency, they were arrested, imprisoned, and could be put to death or sold as slaves to the Etruscans. The terrible scourge of usury provoked a long series of riots from 495 on and a repeated passing of bills.

Several such laws granted a moratorium on debts (delay in payment): for example, in 495 B.C., one such was granted in favor of the debtors who were drafted for the war against the Volsci. On another occasion, the state advanced debtors the wherewithal to acquit themselves of debt, provided that they reimbursed the public treasury at a later date; this virtually amounted to the same as the previous moratorium.

Other laws tended to limit the interest rates. The most famous was the Law of the Twelve Tables (449 B.C.); it fixed the maximum rate at one *uncia* per *libra,* i.e., at 1/12 or 8.33 % (*unciarium foenus*), but no one knows whether this was per month or per year. This has been discussed, and as long as we do not know, it will be hard to appreciate the significance of the measure. A Licinian law of 367 decided that interest already paid by a debtor was to be deducted from the capital, which was equivalent in practice to the elimination of interest. This elimination was also enacted in 342 by the *lex Genucia,* and transgressions of this were severely repressed under the *lex Marcia.* But aside from the Law of the Twelve Tables, these *ad hoc* or demagogic measures soon went out of use.

The Romans also sought to remedy the problem of debt

by extenuating arrest-for-debt; it was not suppressed, but made more of a rarity by the institution of surrendering one's goods. The debtor who yielded all his possessions to his creditors escaped the more severe consequences of insolvency. This resulted from the *lex Poetelia Papiria,* perhaps dated 326. The death penalty and being sold into slavery finally disappeared altogether: imprisonment for debt was retained (up to the present epoch) but without the disastrous outcome of former times.

All these remedies were but palliatives. However, thanks to plunder, and to the colonies where they were settled, indigent Romans drew subsistence from their victories. But the summary procedure whereby the vanquished were despoiled for the benefit of the victors did not establish a real state of equilibrium in Italy, and gradually the peninsula became depopulated. This was already the situation just before the great conquests, and the latter simply brought matters to convulsion point.

B. The Integration of Rome in the Hellenistic Economic Life

At the end of the third century B.C., the Romans lagged behind the Greeks by two or three centuries. Within less than two hundred years, they were to make up for lost time and gain everything they lacked in all aspects of life, whether material, juridical, fiscal, or human.

1. TRANSPORTATION

Land transport was made possible by the construction of the famous Roman roads; their prime object was initially strategic but soon traders traveled them. They fanned out in every direction from Rome. Perhaps the most important was the one which led to Greece. This route was from Rome to Capua along the Via Latina or Via Appia. The latter was extended as far as Brundisium (Brindisi) on the Adriatic; from there on, the traveler crossed a sound of about 75 kilometers width, and then the Via Aegnatia took him from Dyrrachium (Durazzo) to Thessalonica on the Aegean, across Epeiros and Macedonia. Another important road, the Via Flaminia, went north, crossed the Umbrian Mountains and reached the Adriatic at Arriminium or Ariminum (Rimini). From there began the Via Aemilia (which gave its name to the area, Emilia): it took a straight-line path to Milan, marked off every 20 or 30 kilometers by a colony; these colonies were the nuclei of villages still in existence today.

The part played by these roads in commerce was quite limited, however. They crossed too many mountains. Their pavement, very solid but very heavy, rapidly cracked and made transport difficult. Since no one had invented the harnessing and shoeing of horses, the men of ancient times had only two-wheeled carts at their disposal and they had to use two horses to pull a mere 500-kilogram load.

Consequently the main form of transportation was always maritime, despite the fragility of ships and the hazards of navigation. There was a good deal of traveling. Cicero studied in Greece, took refuge there when exiled, and sent his son to study in Athens. St. Paul was an indefatigable traveler. The elimination of piracy by Pompey the Great in 67 B.C. was a considerable help to sailors. The principal ports of Italy were Puteoli, and Brundisium, which profited by the fall of Tarentum. In Rome, the Tiber was equipped with various amenities around 179 B.C.: wharves and warehouses were built along it, and a market was set up and named (from a Greek word) the *Emporium*.

2. THE LEGAL SYSTEM

Ancient Roman law was purely agrarian and quite unsuited to commerce. It excluded from juridical life all slaves, foreigners, and even any son of a family which still had its *pater familias* living. The Romans were unaware of many procedures indispensable to commerce.

Most reforms were due to the praetors, and were brought in during the second and first centuries B.C. In regard to persons, declaration of a *jus gentium,* law common to both Romans and aliens, allowed the latter access to the legal life of Italy. The praetor likewise recognized the existence of a certain contractual role that slaves and sons of families were allowed to play (called *adjectitiae qualitatis*). The Romans may have borrowed from Greek law many procedures which they subsumed under the *jus gentium:* for example, contracts of sale, or hire, deposit, pawnage, mandate, and partnership; and the money loan (*mutuum*), which perhaps appeared somewhat earlier. The praetors organized the bankruptcy procedures (*venditio bonorum*) and determination of the bank balance (*compensatio argentarii*). The Romans also adopted a portion of the maritime law of Rhodes.

Some of the new institutions deserve special mention, such as the bank. The first bankers established in Rome were Greeks. But there were soon to be Roman or Italian *argentarii,* such as the famous family of the Cluvii of Puteoli. They became rich and powerful. The concept of credit also came from Greece. The ancient Romans were hostile to interest loans, and one of them, Cato the Elder (governor of Sardinia), rounded up the usurers: however, later in life he invested part of his own capital in maritime loans. The Romans readily adopted the Greek rate of interest: 1 per cent per month (*centesimae usurae*), with anatocism (interest compounded) from month to month. Those laws, whether old or more recent, which limited the interest rates fell into disuse.

There remained a weak point in this economic system, however, the matter of business companies. Contrary to Greek law, Roman businesses did not constitute "morally responsible individuals." Also, they were rarely permanent enterprises, but just associations of two or three merchants for a limited business project. The only ones of any importance were not truly commercial: these were associations of publicans (tax farmers), public-works contractors, army suppliers, occupiers of public domains. Their associations were powerful and constituted morally responsible units.

3. THE MONETARY SYSTEM

The bronze *as* remained the official coin until about 100 B.C. But it was often devalued: from one *libra,* its weight fell to 1/2, then 1/6, 1/12, 1/24. In 15 B.C. it stabilized at 1/36 *libra.* This devaluation caused a rise in prices, which increased tenfold between the beginning and the end of the Punic Wars, i.e., in a little over one hundred years.

The Romans adopted silver money, the commercial standard of the Hellenistic world. The date of this is controversial; numismatists hesitate between 338 and 267 B.C. Clearly, this silver money had a Greek orientation; the weights of the first coins and the stamped figure were copied from the Greek, the only distinguishing mark being the word "Roma." These coins were probably struck at Capua, the gateway to Magna Graecia. But soon a workshop was set up in Rome, in the Temple of Juno Moneta (the etymology of our word "money"), and original figures were invented for the coins, representing a quadriga (coins called *quadrigats*), a two-wheeled chariot (*bigats*), and victory (*victoriats*). Finally, the unit of silver money became the *denarius,* worth ten *as* (whence its name): but in consequence of the devaluation of the *as,* it was soon worth sixteen *as.* Of the small coins, the most commonly used was the *sestertius,* at first two and one-half *as,* and later four as a result of devaluation of the *as.* The silver coinage was then devalued in its turn, and the *sestertius* became a bronze coin.

The first issue of gold coins took place in 217 B.C., but this was a rare event. Sulla revived this coinage in 87 B.C. It was not until 44 B.C., immediately after Caesar's assassination, that gold coinage became a regular feature, thanks to the resources obtained by pillaging Gaul.

While Roman money had begun by paralleling the Greek, it soon became the leading currency of the Hellenistic world. In the second century B.C., Massilia altered its coinage to make it correspond with the Roman. Numidia did likewise in 105 B.C., after the defeat of Jugurtha. The Attic *drachma* was interchangeable with the Roman *denarius,* even though it in fact weighed 35 centigrams more: Roman prestige ensured a profit to the conqueror.

4. THE BUSINESSMEN

The first merchants to establish themselves in Rome were foreigners: southern Italians, Greeks, Orientals. Lower down the scale there were many freedmen, who often had the advantage of knowing the foreign languages which had been their mother tongues before enslavement. Slaves were employed under their master's names.

The Romans in their turn took up commerce, but they were greedy and brutal rather than clever, and thus aroused hatred against themselves. At the outset of the war with Jugurtha in 112 B.C., all Italians in Cirta were massacred. Twenty-four years later, the war against Mithridates began with the slaughter of 80,000 *negotiatores romani* in Asia, then 20,000 more at Delos.

It was above all the knights who were the businessmen. On the pretext that they ought not to "stoop" to such things, the *lex Claudia* of 218 B.C. had forbidden the nobles to participate in maritime commerce. Another law prohibited them from being publicans. But the laws were often circumvented by intermediaries who lent their names in contracts. The most famous of Roman capitalists must have been the *triumvir* Cassius who went into business with seven million *sestertii* and left 170 millions at his death, despite vast expenditures.

These tycoons imitated the Hellenistic attitude of subordinating everything to money in whatever were its most corrupt aspects. Market-cornering and speculation were continual. One day in 140 B.C. it was discovered that there were quantities of gold in the kingdom of Noricum (present-day Austria). The market price of gold fell by a third at once, only to rebound just as quickly when it was learned that this country was courageously resisting Rome instead of allowing itself to be plundered. Politics and business often interfered with each other. The king of Egypt, Ptolemy Auletes (Cleopatra's father), was dethroned by his subjects. He promised 18,000 talents to Caesar and to Gabinius (proconsul of Syria), if they would reestablish him. This they did. To pay them, Ptolemy took on as finance minister the legal representative of his illustrious creditors, Rabirius Postumus, who then behaved so extortionately that the king finally imprisoned him. Once released, he was prosecuted in Rome for extortion, as was Gabinius. Cicero pleaded on his behalf and got him acquitted.

C. Exploitation of Conquest

As conquerors, the Romans indulged in a brutal and cynical exploitation, not only of the vanquished, but also of certain of their allies and of countries who still remained free. It was a real spoliation. This exploitation was sometimes legal, to the profit of the state, sometimes illegal but tolerated, to the profit of certain private individuals.

1. official exploitation for state profit

As long as war lasted, the costs weighed as heavily on Rome's allies as on herself. When she was victorious, the vanquished sometimes extricated themselves by paying an indemnity. But in case of total defeat and capitulation, the victor had all the rights. No rules of war in ancient times required one to spare subjects, even nonbelligerents, or to refrain from taking the enemy's property. The amount of portable booty taken was considerable: Caesar's conquest of Gaul enabled so much gold to be acquired that its price dropped in the ratio of 11 to 7, and it was soon possible to strike a coinage from it. But there was worse to come.

The Romans enslaved the enemy and maintained their lands: estates of conquered kings, sites of cities they destroyed, such as Carthage and Corinth, and often part of the land (the best, of course) of the vanquished hitherto spared. This vast "heritage" (which was not mobile) became the *ager publicus,* state property. The state ran the mines, by means of slaves. The arable lands were divided into two parts: the smaller quantity was allotted to the Romans along with full property rights—either parceled out to individuals or, more often, by establishing a colony, which divided land amongst its members; the remainder was leased, or handed over with a more or less precarious title deed, to those already *in situ* (*agri occupatorii*), who were more often than not the original owners of the land and were now subject to rent dues. This situation, of which the law pretended to be unaware, lasted for a long time.

Rome also seized men, in conformity with the ancient rules of war, which she enforced in all their harshness; she took not only prisoners of war, but also many civilians. The result was that veritable herds of slaves were sent off to Italy: 150,000 in 167 B.C. after the victory in Macedonia; 50,000 in 146 B.C. after the capture of Carthage. This was the time when the slave-based society was formed, a feature of the centuries to follow.

Rome took yet more money, even from its allies. Sulla expelled Mithridates from the Province of Asia in 85 B.C., and then quartered his troops there, making the cities responsible for their pay. He raised the pay immediately, and also imposed on these cities a war contribution of 20,000 talents. As for the vanquished, they were forced to pay war indemnities: Carthage (in 201 B.C.) was charged 10,000 talents; Antiocheia, in Syria, 15,000 in 190 B.C.

There were also permanent tributes, simultaneous taxes and rentals on lands reserved by Rome as her own property. They bore various names: *vectigal, stipendium, tributum,* tithes. These were sometimes old established taxes enforced and collected thenceforth for the benefit of the Roman state; sometimes they were new impositions based on the rights of conquest. Cicero, in his prosecution of Verres, gives interesting details about the regime in Sicily. The Sicilians were first of all paying what can be properly called a tax—a tithe of the wheat harvested (*frumentum decumanum*), and collected in kind; the same on wine, oil, and other products. Before the conquest, this tax dated back to a law of Hiero II (Hieron), tyrant of Syracuse, in the third century. Besides this, Rome commandeered wheat (*frumentum emptum*) and paid for it at a price fixed by a unilateral decision of the Senate. Lastly, the Sicilians had to provide wheat for the residence of the Roman governor.

Rome sometimes also imposed on conquered countries an economic regime designed exclusively for her own profit. She forbade viticulture and olive-growing in Gallia Narbonensis, to protect Italian production. She also kept for herself the overall monopoly of gold coinage, almost always that of silver, and sometimes even of bronze. Athens was one of the few cities privileged to keep its own coinage.

2. EXTORTIONS BY INDIVIDUALS

A whole swarm of exploiters were soon to descend on the provinces occupied by the Roman army. First there were the merchants (*negotiatores*), scarcely distinguishable from loan sharks, come to offer their services to cities crushed by taxes and by contributions to the costs of war. When not repaid, they gained the cooperation of full Roman power to seize goods and reduce the debtors to slavery. The town of Salamis, capital of Cyprus, had borrowed 50 talents from a man named Scaptius, at 4 per cent per month (48 per cent per annum), with the usual monthly compounding of interest. When Scaptius was not paid, he had himself nominated commander of a troop of cavalry by the Roman governor of Cilicia, to which Cyprus belonged. With his troop, Scaptius then besieged the local Senate, five members of which died of starvation. Cicero was named proconsul of Cilicia in 50 B.C. and learned of this. Greatly shocked, he reduced interest rates to 1 per cent per month, converting monthly anatocism to yearly; compound interest was only computed on the simple interest of one whole year. At this new rate, which was applied retroactively over the six years elapsed since the loan was made, the debt still amounted to the appreciable sum of 106 talents. Yet, not satisfied with this, Scaptius then revealed that he was but a "front man" for Brutus (one of Julius Caesar's murderers-to-be), the friend and political colleague of Cicero. The much-embarrassed Cicero hedged for a time and finally left the province without settling the problem.

Another category of exploiter was that of the publicans. As in France in the time of Louis XIV, tax collection was leased out to farmers-general, the publicans: they immediately deposited a forfeit with the state, and undertook to collect the taxes. But they appropriated considerable sums over and above the amounts due: this was tolerated in consideration of the fact that they had to cover expenses and make a profit. But no limit was ever set to this supplement; no one had any chance of success by resorting to litigation because, when a tax-payer complained, the judge assigned by the governor to resolve the dispute was always another publican.

Lastly, governors of provinces and their assistants indulged in all kinds of injustices and extortions, grabbing whatever came within reach, be it money or works of art. They were led into this mode of behavior by the policy of recruitment itself: as Roman magistrates, ruined financially by the demagogic expenses of their electoral campaign, they went off to recover their fortunes in some province, to the detriment of its inhabitants. This we know from Cicero, who had bitterly reproached Verres, governor of Sicily; but he himself followed this by defending many other governors accused, quite deservedly, of similar crimes; and, when governor of Cilicia, he was to make a considerable profit from his position, in spite of his honesty and respect for law.

Nevertheless, attempts were made to remedy these abuses. At least seven laws were passed, between 149 and 59 B.C., to organize legal procedures of *repetundae pecuniae* to recover the money and to make extortionate governors disgorge their exactions. These laws only resulted in fiasco. Senators and knights wrangled over places on the juries responsible for deciding the cases, so as to favor in turn the provincial governors or publicans of their own social class. Verdicts depended solely on whether the jury was composed of friends or enemies of the accused, and were often scandalous. The lieutenant-governor of Asia, Rutilius Rufus, resisted the publicans, and was then condemned in Rome by a jury of knights. He withdrew to Smyrna, the home of his alleged victims, and lived there honored by all. Only under the Empire was effective supervision established.

The result of all these forms of exploitation was vast revenue for Rome. In 167 B.C. the Romans, having seized the fabulous treasure of the king of Macedonia, were able to eliminate the direct taxation they themselves paid and never restored it. The state budget doubled at once, increasing from 100 to 200 million *sestertii,* after the kingdom of Pergamum was annexed in 130 B.C. Pompey boasted of having raised it to 340 million after the conquest of Syria in 63 B.C.

But the provinces were pillaged and a portion of the labor force was led off into slavery, while Roman colonies were settled on the best land. There was ruin everywhere. Cicero paints a dramatic picture of Sicilian villages deserted by their inhabitants, their population being reduced by more than two-fifths in three years. The Roman conquest reduced much wealth to poverty, not to mention powerful cities like Corinth, Carthage, or Tarentum, which were completely razed, along with the industries carried on there.

D. Repercussions in Italy

Although pillage enriched certain Romans, it was far from profiting everyone. An economic crisis exhausted Italy and provoked violent social unheavals.

1. ECONOMIC CRISIS

The agrarian revolution began in the third century, and worsened along the same lines as it had previously done in Greece. Italy suffered competition from wheat granaries abroad: Sicily, Cisalpine Gaul, Spain, Carthaginian Africa, and even the region of the present-day Ukraine. In 202 B.C., imports of Sicilian wheat were on such a scale that prices collapsed; unable to sell, the merchants abandoned them to the shippers to pay off freight charges. Cicero said at that time that the wheat of Sicily alone was enough to feed all Italy. In addition, farmers gave up wheat-farming for arboriculture: vines, olive trees, and fruit trees; the first century B.C. was when the cherry was introduced into Europe, originally from Kerasunde, a town in Asia Minor on the Pontus Euxinus; from there the cherry was brought to Italy by the famous gourmet Lucullus, who had waged war against Mithridates in that area. But this kind of farming demanded much care and often suffered from slumps, and the time was not far off when farmers were to abandon it in their turn in favor of large-scale cattle-raising.

There were also changes in the structure of agriculture as a business. The Roman small farmers were ruined by the wars, by mobilization and by the slaughter involved; by competition from new lands; and lastly by competition from the abundant slave labor dumped in Italy. They sold their lands, which were immediately bought by the rich. In this way vast estates (*latifundia*) were established everywhere, of which Pliny was later to write that they had ruined Italy. They were likewise established on the *ager publicus,* and portioned off in large allottments to the publicans. On these *latifundia,* cultivation was carried out by slaves who were kept on the minimum living standard, in the strictest sense of the words, and were forced to remain celibate to eliminate every unnecessary mouth. Cato the Elder (d. 149 B.C.) had an 85-hectare estate in Campania planted with vines and olive trees, and cultivated by 29 slaves, all celibate: yet before Cato, seventeen families had lived by wheat-farming on that same area of land. Concentration of property is therefore clearly in evidence. In addition to this, the large-scale owner was an absentee landlord. Tiberius Gracchus, while crossing Etruria in 135 B.C., gained the impression that it was an empty country, where one met nobody except occasionally a gang of slaves. This slave regime upset all the factors involved in production, which had been organized for centuries on the basis of superabundant, low-cost labor.

As for Italy's industrial production, it stagnated in a state of mediocrity. Metallurgy, which was continued in Etruria and Campania, underwent no further development. In Rome itself, there was no industry beyond building-construction and manufacture of luxury articles such as jewelry.

Furthermore, the balance of trade was unfavorable. Of the Mediterranean world, now in the process of unification, the whole western part behaved like a young or undeveloped country, exporting raw materials and importing manufactured items from the East. But in this western part, Rome was conspicuous in that she did not even export raw materials; she exported virtually nothing, and Italy herself little enough; while she imported not only manufactured goods but also foodstuffs. The trade deficit was made up by taxes, tribute, and interest on loans; that is, Rome paid for her purchases in the provinces with the money she extorted from them. She lived in luxury without producing anything utilitarian, and her economy was unhealthy.

2. SOCIAL CRISIS

All the disheartened farmers who left the country became stranded on the streets of Rome, but found no work there and became the hard-core unemployed, the mob of the run-down sections of town, always stirred up, ready for every *coup-de-main* and civil war. Many measures were considered in an attempt to remedy the situation. It is difficult to put the debt-reduction laws under this heading (Sulla's in 88 B.C. cut their debts by three-fourths at one stroke); this is because debtors were mainly to be found in the upper classes, notably among politicians committed to rivaling each other's electoral promises. The debt problem was therefore more political than social.

Among those remedies tried, one naïve or demagogic procedure was to enact the sumptuary laws whose object was to force the *gens* to reduce expenditure (*sumptus* in Latin means "expense") in order to restore the old Roman ideal of frugality to a place of honor. Many of these laws appeared successively between *ca.* 200 B.C. through the reign of Augustus; but Tiberius refused to propose a new one. One of the oldest, soon repealed, forbade women to wear jewelry in the street or to go out in a carriage. Others aimed at restricting expenditure on meals: not more than 10 *sestertii* per head for an ordinary meal, and 30 for holidays, by the law of 161 B.C.; these figures rose to 200 and 300 *sestertii* under Augustus, with an upper limit of 1,000 for a wedding feast. This huge increase shows how much the laws were a failure.

The corn laws were more in earnest. As early as the fourth century, in times of exceptional shortage, the state had bought corn abroad for cheap resale at home. This precedent, renewed more and more frequently, ended by becoming the most regular of institutions. The first step in this direction was the *lex Sempronia frumentaria* proposed by Caius Gracchus, and passed. This law organized a complete policy of transportation and storage of wheat, and gave every Roman citizen the right to receive a certain amount of wheat at an official price (a reduced one, of course). The law was revived and improved repeatedly around 100 B.C. and then again in 78 B.C. The second step was taken in 58: it was decided that citizens should now receive free wheat. The result was unexpected. The few farmers remaining in the country left it to live in Rome without working. Masters freed their slaves so that the latter, now Roman citizens, would be fed at state expense. About 45 B.C., Caesar found that there were 320,000 beneficiaries of this free-distribution system, almost 1 Roman citizen in every 3. He reduced the number to 150,000, but it began to increase again; the empire later inherited the problem, and had no better success in finding the answer.

The Popular party clamored for land redistribution, particularly in the case of the *ager publicus* (which had been cornered by the well-to-do) and also for redistribution of the *latifundia*. They supported their demand by the precedent (real or imaginary) of the Licinian laws of 367 B.C. which, it was said, had forbidden the possession of more than 500 *jugera* per family. The first agrarian law was proposed by Tiberius Gracchus, tribune of the people in 134 B.C. Struck by the deserted state of the Etrurian countryside, he revived the provisions of the Licinian laws, with some minor changes. This *lex Sempronia agraria* was passed the following year and brought back the traditional limitation on landowners of the *ager publicus* of 500 *jugera,* raised by 250 *jugera* per son of the family. The remainder of the land was to be reclaimed by the state and distributed in the form of inalienable lots of 30 *jugera* to the landless, in return for rent (*vectigal*) paid to the state. But Tiberius Gracchus fell foul of the bitter opposition of the rich. To get his law passed, he had to bring off two coups d'etat in succession. The second time he provoked a riot in which he perished. Nevertheless the law was enforced to some extent, at least in southern Italy, as inscriptions bear witness.

Caius Gracchus, Tiberius' brother, became tribune in his turn six years later. In addition to his corn law, he proposed new agrarian measures. His great idea was to found colonies on the sites of destroyed cities, such as Carthage, Tarentum, and Corinth. After some degree of success, he too was assassinated in 121 B.C. The Sempronian laws were then nibbled away by a series of piecemeal measures which deprived them of all effectiveness, and towards 100 B.C., it could be stated that there were no more than 2,000 landed proprietors all told.

The concept of agrarian legislation was in the air and it persisted, however, although Cicero wrecked an agrarian proposal during his consulate (63 B.C.), Marius (*ca.* 100), Sulla (*ca.* 80), and then Caesar (59 B.C.) each adopted one. Those of Sulla and Caesar were no longer social, but partisan. Land was not taken from those who owned too much, but from their political opponents who were on the proscription lists and from the Italian cities which were their allies. The beneficiaries of redistribution were no longer the poor, but victorious veterans of the civil wars. Sulla's agrarian law was a great success: 120,000 of his soldiers were settled. The others' laws had only average success. The new settlers, for lack of livestock and experience, and doubtless also of any real desire to return to the land, in many cases preferred to return to Rome; here they took their place once more in its degenerate political milieu, ready for anything.

CHAPTER THREE

The Early Roman Empire (Le Haut-Empire)

The period that begins after the battle of Actium with the reign of Augustus is the sequel and, in many respects, the prolongation of the Hellenistic. This period corresponds to the political regime called the Early Empire or Principate; but it is usual to consider the Early Empire period as the three centuries from Actium to the beginning of Diocletian's reign (A.D. 284), even though the last fifty years of chronic anarchy scarcely deserve the name Haut-Empire with its eulogistic implications. In regard to economics, the picture is more accurate if one cuts off this half-century of decadence so as to join it on to the Later Empire (Bas-Empire) of which it is clearly the forerunner.

The Early Empire, thus reduced to some 260 years, marks the climax of the evolution of economics in antiquity. But the collapse which was to follow was already heralded by two kinds of prior indications: the first kind reveals the weakness of this flourishing economy; the second group involves changes which foreshadow the systems of the Later Empire, without arousing adverse comment.

I. THE ECONOMIC APOGEE

Various factors contributed to this high level: peace and unity of a huge empire; great public works; an honorable administration, with responsible governors, and publicans closely watched, until they were finally eliminated altogether. With the exception of Egypt, the provinces were no longer exploited, and progressively more of their inhabitants were to become Roman citizens.

Another factor helping to create prosperity was monetary stability, almost perfect over two centuries from Augustus to Commodus. The unit of coinage was the *sestertius,* henceforth a simple bronze piece. However, the largest transactions made use of the silver *denarius* (worth 4 *sestertii*). Augustus also issued a gold piece, the *aureus* of 7.27 grams (making 45 in the *libra* of 327 grams). The *aureus* was equivalent to 25 *denarii* or 100 *sestertii.* Of these three, the basic coin from now on was to be the *aureus,* and one may say that the empire worked on a system of gold monometallism, a new phenomenon in history; in the Hellenistic period, silver was predominant. In fact, when the ratio of silver to gold varied, the gold piece remained constant and the *denarius* changed in value. This ratio was 1:12 under Augustus, and fell to 1:9 in Trajan's time, due to the conquest of Dacia and the capture of the treasure of King Decebalus.

Small devaluations occurred in Nero's time and especially after Marcus Aurelius'; they subsequently became worse. They began with a reduction in the purity grade of silver pieces; the percentage of alloy additive rose from 2 to 25 per cent, then to 30 and 40 per cent. Then the actual weights of the coins were reduced. These manipulations were the probable cause of a rise in prices, to counter which Commodus decreed a maximum. The landslide was hardly perceptible at first but became headlong in Caracalla's time, the second decade of the third century A.D. It was to do nothing but gain momentum as the century proceeded.

A. Commercial Expansion

The imperial economy exhibited expansion most markedly in the area of commerce. Goods were transported over very large distances, even the heaviest, and among them foodstuffs. Wine, oil, and above all wheat now gave rise, not to occasional shipments as previously, but to regular, large-scale trade such as had never been seen in ancient times, and was never to disappear in the centuries that followed. Further, manufactured items and raw materials circulated from one end of the empire to the other and sometimes even beyond.

Transportation within the empire was primarily maritime, and the Mediterranean was her axis. Great public works were undertaken in the construction and improvement of harbors; moles were thrown up, lighthouses built, and even artificial islands created; docks and union canals were dug out. Roman technology only failed at one point: how to stop the silting-up of certain harbors; among the most important were Rome, Ostia, and Ephesos, which Strabo called "the most important trade-market of all Asia."

Most Mediterranean rivers were not navigable; the only important ones were the peripheral rivers: the Nile, Euphrates, Rhine, and Danube. In the case of Gaul, Strabo noted the fortunate arrangement of the water courses which allowed transportation along three principal axes: Rhône-Saône-Seine; Aude and Garonne via the Naurouze corridor; and the Loire.

The Romans, renowned for their great construction feats, did little canal-building. Vespasian sent Jewish prisoners to cut through the Isthmus of Corinth, but without success. Trajan had the Nile–Red Sea canal dredged again, but it was hardly ever used.

No previous empire, even the Persian, had built so many roads and bridges. The Roman road-network was so solidly constructed that it lasted into and beyond the Middle Ages; both mountains and deserts were crossed. Although overland transport was not the most important, it, too, contributed to commercial expansion.

Commerce beyond the empire was likewise important, but it was based almost entirely on luxury goods, with the exception of the wheat bought from Scythia (the present-day Ukraine). Trade followed three main directions. From the North, the Romans imported the Baltic Sea amber, furs and slaves via the roads which converged at the far end of the Adriatic or on the shores of the Pontus Euxinus. Roman coins have been found as far as Latvia and southern Sweden. The Germans, who had no money, used Roman coins, preferable to the old fashioned ones to which they were accustomed. From central Africa, either via Egypt or the Saharan trails converging on Leptis Magna, came ivory, gold, Negro slaves, and valuable woods. This was the period when the camel, long known in Asia, made its appearance in Africa. But the most important trade was with the Far East. Rome imported a wide variety of wares, all luxury items: perfumes, pearls and precious stones, spices such as pepper, and above all, silk. She paid for these in wine, and in coral fished from the Mediterranean to the point where there was no more to be found. Augustus and Trajan received ambassadors from India. Roman coins and pottery have been found on the Malabar Coast of southern India. From A.D. 160 on, men knew of a "Chersonesus Aurea" (the Malacca peninsula). Trajan once received a Chinese ambassador, and the Annals of the Chinese Emperors refer to the arrival of envoys from a Western king called "An-toon" in A.D. 166: this obviously refers to Marcus Aurelius Antoninus.

B. The Progress of Agriculture

Large-scale production of wheat was developed in Egypt, in Africa (present-day Tunisia), Sicily and, to a lesser extent, Spain. Rome also obtained wheat from Scythia. Market gardening and arboriculture also made progress. The olive tree and vine continued to spread, and people began to cultivate new kinds of fruit imported from Persia, such as the apricot and the peach, whose name (*persica*) bears witness to its origin.

Above all else the empire brought new and underdevel- oped land into cultivation. Forests were cleared, marshlands drained, deserts irrigated. There are Roman ruins in certain areas of Syria which are now deserted, and the contrast is so great that some have been able to believe that a change in climate has taken place since then; very probably a mistaken view. Colonies were founded on the high plateaus of North Africa. But the West was the main area of development: the chestnut tree spread through Gaul and still more the vine, especially in Bordelais and Bourgogne, as it did on the banks of the Rhine and Moselle rivers. The map showing the vine-growing areas in contemporary Germany coincides with the same map under the Roman Empire.

Many treatises on agronomy were written in the first century A.D. Columella's is the best known.

C. Industry

Industrial expansion was the least noteworthy of the three. Technological progress was poor and was disregarded: the water mill was known, but seldom used; so was the cask, but fragile ceramic jars were preferred. Under Vespasian, when the obelisk was erected in Rome (present-day Piazza San Pietro), an inventor suggested an engineering technique which would have greatly facilitated the operation; but the emperor preferred manual slave labor so as not to leave slaves unemployed.

Mass production appeared at this time but the quality was vulgar. Although we cannot speak of heavy industry in the modern sense, we should note the existence of workshops comprising several hundred workers and selling their products far and wide by means of agents scattered abroad. The same is true for cheap plates and dishes or clothes for the poorer class. Some of these workshops are famous, such as the Arretium (Arezzo) tableware factory, the coppersmith's workshops in Campania, whose products reached the shores of the Baltic, or the oil-lamp shops of the Fortis family in Mutina (Modena), specimens of which are still preserved in all our museums.

The East was always the leader in production, but one can see a tendency toward improvement in the West. The mines of Spain and more especially of Gaul were being worked intensively. Building developed in characteristic manner: Italy had been building in durable materials for a long time; in the first century A.D., the concrete house had replaced the shanty in Gaul; in the second century the concrete house reached the Rhineland and the Danube. Of the new countries, Gaul progressed the furthest, relatively speaking: she had a metallurgical industry, a remarkable locksmith and metalwork industry, and active pottery works; it was Gaul that made the cheap woolen clothing worn by the common people of Rome herself.

II. ECONOMIC AND GEOGRAPHICAL IMBALANCE

The brilliant features of the economy cannot, however, hide the imbalances, economic or geographical, which tended to worsen all the more because the imperial government lacked the general grasp of affairs needed to remedy them; it confined itself to maintaining the existing state of affairs on an ad hoc basis, and in case of absolute necessity carried out some timid reform designed, not to adapt to changes, but to reestablish as early as possible the status quo.

A. Imbalance Between Production and Consumption

Agricultural production stagnated, especially in wheat, which supplied the basic food. The reason was that, to feed Rome cheaply, the price was artificially held too low by requisitioning. Farmers who managed to escape this preferred to produce oil or wine. Domitian banned the planting of new vines in Italy as a cure-all.

On the other hand, the consumers, especially townsmen, were privileged and hard to please. Many did no work. Towns were flourishing, but were perhaps too numerous and too heavily populated for the productive capacities and transportation system of the ancient world; they were therefore constantly threatened by shortages. Also, there was perhaps too great a display of luxury, and unproductive waste: feast days, games, and building of monuments. Furthermore, Rome must be set apart from the other cities—Aymard called her "a monstrous city for that period." She may have had a population of the order of one million, though an exact figure is hard to arrive at. The proud ideal of the Conquering City, mistress of the world, and the uneasiness of the government in face of this idle, greedy mob incited by continual intrique, combined to turn her citizens into recipients of relief, so to speak, fed at low prices and stupefied with public entertainments. *Panem et circenses* [bread and circuses] were what they demanded. A large-scale commissariat, the *annona,* was organized in the period spanned by Augustus and Claudius. At its head was an official, the prefect of the *annona.* About 200,000 heads of families were supplied with a kind of ration card and received free wheat. A special fleet was assigned to its transportation. The great public works involved in providing the wharves of the Tiber river and the port of Ostia were simply to enable ships of this fleet to dock. The shipowners and the bakers, and all who took part in feeding the capital city received privileges from the emperor. To complete the official effort, still inadequate, each one of innumerable plebeians (called a *cliens*) received every day the *sportula* [dole] of his patrician patron.

The other cities of the empire were not so well favored. The wheat of Egypt, Sicily, and Africa was reserved for Rome, and the wheat of Scythia for the Danube army. There remained little enough of the means of subsistence for the other recipients. Thus the Greek cities often went hungry. They created special magistrates and *leitourgia* [liturgies], charging the rich with the job of finding a way to feed their fellow citizens at their own expense.

B. Geographical Imbalance

First of all, there was a state of imbalance between old and new lands, the first in the East, the second mainly in the West. Most of the eastern provinces were rich and prosperous, and in the first rank of them was Egypt, wheat granary of the ancient world. Tacitus tells us that, during the civil war which was to win him the empire, Vespasian, master of Egypt, could have won without a battle simply by placing an embargo on wheat bound for Italy, which it fed for a third of the year. This land was exploited in the same way as under the Ptolemies.

In the West, Sicily remained rich, and African agriculture was important. But the rest of it, often heavily forested, was underdeveloped. Progress here was certainly continuous, but the arrears could not be made up all at once. Spain never attained prosperity. Britain and that portion of Germany which the Romans succeeded in subjecting were merely under a military occupation. Gaul alone of these new lands was forging ahead but, except for Lyon and the southern region, the towns, still quite small, mark the limits of this development.

A new phenomenon, however, appeared after the second century A.D.: the development of the Rhine-Danube region, which became a direct trade route from Asia Minor to the North Sea. But this was the beginning of a new imbalance, because the northern regions aimed at superiority over the Mediterranean axis about which the empire revolved.

In reality, Greece and Italy were in an advanced state of decay. Once it had been cereals, now it was arboriculture, which, facing fierce competition, began to be abandoned. Much of the land returned to pasturage and to waste. The decline of Magna Graecia, where harvests had once been rich, was now final, for this area has never recovered. Possibly the land has been exhausted.

As for industry, the mines of Greece produced virtually nothing more. Italian production, still fairly flourishing in the first century, was kept going with difficulty. For example, the Arretium ceramic industry suffered from Gallic competition. Trade presents the same picture. Italian merchants had recently spread throughout the whole Hellenistic world. Under the empire, retreat was the order of the day. Juvenal could write that "The Orontes is flowing into the Tiber," and besides the Syrian, there were African, Spanish, and Gallic merchants. From the second century on, the Rhine-Danube route became a partial substitute for the Mediterranean seaway.

The emperors sometimes tried to respond to the situation. Domitian first forbade the planting of new vines in Italy and then ordered the uprooting of half those in the provinces. This overly simple protectionism, not officially abandoned until A.D. 280, had the sole result of arousing complaints. Trajan undertook another draining of the Pontine marshes and forced the senators to invest a third of their capital in Italian lands. These measures clearly could not retrieve the situation.

C. Imbalance of Trade with the Far East

Rome imported from the Far East—and to an increasing extent—wares whose high price her exports could not cover. She was forced to settle her account by payments in gold. Tiberius denounced before the Senate the custom of wearing silk and gems for which, he said, "We are carrying the Empire's treasure to strangers or enemies." The Senate then banned men from wearing silk. But a little later, Pliny valued the annual loss of specie to India, Arabia, and China as 100 million *sestertii*. It was to lay hands on her gold that Trajan conquered Dacia.

All these imbalances had their political repercussions. According to one of the most eminent economic historians, Rostovtzeff, the Antonines, in order to allow the towns to grow, oppressed the peasants by a policy of continual requisitions. Under pressure from the army, which was recruited in the country, the Severan dynasty marked a period of reversal and struck terror into the upper-middle class, urban and rural alike. There may be some truth in this theory. The same applies to foreign policy. If conquest ceased immediately after Trajan, it was because the coffers were almost empty. But the Romans soon had to defend themselves, either by costly wars, or by buying peace from the barbarians by turning over tribute to them. The equilibrium of the empire was soon upset: by the end of the second century devaluation of the coinage reappeared, and in the third, the political structure became much weakened.

III. INTERNAL TRANSFORMATIONS

Although not themselves being factors making for imbalance, significant transformations occurred under the Early Empire that foreshadowed some of the features characteristic of the period to come. These transformations concerned business structure and the status of manual labor.

A. Tendency toward Business Mergers

Gradually the smaller enterprises, especially agricultural, passed from the hands of small operators or growers to the big landowners and the state. The agrarian laws, designed to eliminate the *latifundia,* failed completely. Only one more (short-lived) was to be passed, under Nerva. *Latifundia* seemed to multiply, not only to the profit of individuals, but also of the temples, cities, and the state. In addition to agricultural enterprise, workshops, forges, and the weaving industry were sometimes also included. In Nero's reign, half the province of Africa belonged to only six landowners: Nero condemned them to death and confiscated their property. We are forced to believe that the result was not conclusive because, in the middle of the third century A.D., St. Cyprian, bishop of Carthage, could write: "The rich add estate to estate. They chase the poor from their borders and their lands extend beyond measure or limit."

But the state itself "has become the greatest latifundiarist in the Empire." [1] Augustus, like Ptolemy Philadelphus before him, seized the property of all Egypt's temples, instituting a religious budget in compensation. Another means of extending the imperial domains was confiscation. Every time there was a civil war, the state victimized the losers in this way and, in the intervals between, many rich landowners were condemned to have their property confiscated and to undergo corporal punishment on charges of conspiracy (real or alleged), as under Nero for example. All these estates were organized to form autonomous units (*fundus* or *saltus*) each with its own charter (*lex fundi*); each was headed by an official, the *procurator,* controlled by a centralized administration.

These "nationalizations" (to use a modern term) extended also to mines and quarries. Augustus, in his fight against the publicans, made all mines a state monopoly. But Trajan revoked this to attract capital investment to them, although the state held on to a number of them nevertheless. They too were organized under a charter—that relating to the Vipasca copper mine in Portugal, and dating from Hadrian's time, has been preserved—and were entrusted to the management of a *procurator*. The work was done either by slaves or by those condemned to forced labor, comparable to slaves. The state likewise created military workshops for arms manufacture, and the army itself undertook public works, dug quarries and built camps and colonies.

This progressive nationalization did not only extend to ownership of the means of production but also to the methods

[1] A. Piganiol, *Histoire de Rome* (1954), p. 281.

of cultivation. More and more, farm-leasing was abandoned, as much to improve state lands as to enable it to manage its own affairs. The publicans or farmers-general, who more often than not subdivided the work amongst underfarmers, were at first strictly controlled and then gradually eliminated. They were replaced by small-scale tax farmers operating single-handedly. As for taxes, the towns and villages came to be responsible for their collection, and for this they had to employ municipal functionaries and magistrates. The mines and workshops were state managed.

B. Changes in the Status of Farm Laborers

Gradually, as their conquests extended, the Romans eliminated almost everywhere the various systems analogous to the serfdom of our Middle Ages. On the other hand, they made slavery a widespread affair. Under the empire, the reverse trend occurred. Slavery tended to diminish, for lack of a new group of great victories to revive it, and enfranchisements reduced the size of the existing slave pool. On the other hand, short-term farm rental (a customary five years) on a freehold basis underwent a crisis: Pliny the Younger had difficulty in finding tenant farmers, and those he found were hard put to pay off their dues. In place of these two traditional procedures, we see the appearance of tenures characterized, despite great diversity, by two features: long-term leases, hereditary and virtually perpetual; and low rent, usually consisting of a certain fraction of the products paid in kind, and in the corvées. These tenancies were set up on city lands and on land belonging to private individuals or to the public treasury. They are known to us by inscriptions in North Africa (at Henchir-Mettich, Ain-Wassel, Ain-el-Djemala, Soukh-el-Khmis). Tenancies were controlled by administrative regulations (*lex Pertinax, lex Manciana, lex Hadriana,* etc.); since they aimed mainly at uncultivated or abandoned land, they allowed any who wished to buy to occupy and cultivate them in conformity with the prescribed rules, and to plant certain stated crops, while granting rights of possession and hereditary usufruct of the land (*ius possidendi ac fruendi heredique suo relinquendi*).

C. Development of Corporative Bodies

Groups of artisans, petty merchants or craftsmen (*collegia* or *corpora*) developed, thanks to the constitutional liberty granted under a law of Augustus'. Some were favored by the administration. Their progress was nevertheless very variable, depending on the region and the profession in question. They were to be found mainly in Italy and southern Gaul, to a much lesser extent in Greece and the Orient, and hardly at all in Africa. The most numerous and important were those involving food supplies (guilds of ship chandlers, *navicularii,* were powerful), while they were rarer in other trades. Their aim at this period was more moral than economic. As yet there were no guilds for protection of the profession and for apprenticeship, such as the guilds of the Middle Ages were to be, but they were syndicates of humble folk, or brotherhoods uniting their members by the bonds of friendship and mutual aid. They were protected by some powerful patrons who presented them with gifts and assured them political support. This phenomenon, although still of limited importance, developed increasingly and became a considerable asset to economic life in the course of the third century.

CHAPTER FOUR

The Later Roman Empire

From the economic point of view, one can view the Later Empire as beginning around the middle of the third century. In the West, the catastrophic invasions and the collapse of the empire mark its end in the second half of the fifth century A.D.; in the East, it lasted a century longer, until the end of the reign of Justinian (527–65). These three centuries were marked by a severe economic crisis and by the first system of planned economy to be carried out over so vast a territory.

I. THE ECONOMIC CRISIS

Many brilliant features still characterized the Later Empire, notably the extent of foreign trade. Two facts will give an idea of its abundance: the price of silk, reckoned in stable currency (or by weight), dropped by about 75 per cent between the third and fourth centuries; in A.D. 410, when Rome was sacked, the Visigoths found 5,000 pounds of pepper in the bonded warehouses. Moreover, there was a great deal of wealth in evidence. It was only in the fifth century, and almost solely in the West, that the crisis reached dramatic proportions but it was latent and often serious throughout the period in general.

A. Crisis in Agricultural Production

Although industry was scarcely affected, farm production was clearly inadequate and was declining. Nevertheless, one must distinguish one region from another in this matter. Syria and Asia Minor were very prosperous, but Greece and Italy were undergoing economic depression. In Campania itself, once so fertile, Honorius in A.D. 395 struck from the tax register 130,000 hectares which had become desert. Malaria spread in Tuscany. Even Egypt was adversely affected by what seems to have been a cyclic phenomenon in her history. Each regime exploited and exhausted her in turn. The villages of El Fayum were covered once more by the desert sands. The causes of this situation are sought in vain. In the absence of statistical data, one cannot verify the demographic hypotheses, which assume a drop in population. It is also possible to think of political causes: wars, invasions, and an excess of fiscal laws both too burdensome and inappropriately applied to the various classes.

Transformations occurred in the agricultural system. There were, it is true, many villages of free peasants, but the system of large estates (*fundus, villa*) continued to expand, till these estates became a significant feature of the Later Empire. They often belonged to well-to-do private individuals, but the imperial demesne continued to expand as a result of confiscations. The emperor also took over the administration of the goods of pagan temples and of cities. The Christian church from A.D. 321 had the right to receive endowments and legacies, and since she virtually never refused one, her revenues from benefices became significant in this period.

Three features characterized the domain of the Later Empire: extent, autarchy, and juridical privilege. One could give a long list of whole villages which bore their lord's name, often to be discovered in today's toponymy: how many Martignés or Martignys are perpetuating the memory of some

Martinus right up to our own times, and Savignys or Sévignes a Sabinus family? These large landowners were organized for survival in a largely closed economy. In contrast to Cato the Elder, who bought his goods in the town, the agronomist Palladius at the end of the fourth century recommended having all crafts on the premises to avoid all purchases if possible. Quite frequently, several different workshops operated on the estate. The bakehouse and the common-or-garden mill could already be found there. Finally, this *de facto* autonomy was sometimes paralleled by a *de jure* autonomy, owing to usurpations in the realm of justice or of taxation; sometimes owing to small private armies and to the privileges that individuals, especially the influential members (*potentes*) of the senatorial class, wrung from the imperial government.

Absentee landlordism disappeared. The lord frequently lived on his estate. Around his home was a reserve (*indominicatum*) cultivated by means of corvées imposed on the tenants. The remainder, which was the greater part of the estate, was distributed as small allotments to colonists, theoretically freehold, or to *casati,* "settled" slaves to whom had been given a small house and a strip of land to farm, in exchange for dues and corvée service. The social ranks were thus brought closer together within the lower class, that of the *humiliores,* although this method of farming produced, paradoxically enough, "the union of large-scale landownership and small-scale farming" (Piganiol). On the other hand, legislation brought into being another kind of land tenure, under the Greek name *emphuteusis;* this kind was *in perpetuo* or virtually so, and aimed at bringing uncultivated land into operation.

B. Monetary Crisis

The crisis of the Later Empire was certainly not the first inflation in history, but was the first to proceed rapidly and to be comparable to those our own period has experienced.

The basic cause lay in the overexpenditure of a state in a desperate plight.

A slow rate of deterioration continued from the end of the second century A.D. The rate increased under Caracalla, around A.D. 215, and became a landslide in 256 under Valerian, accompanying military defeat on all sides. Aurelian's attempt at stabilization (*ca.* A.D. 270) had only transient results. At the end of the third century, the gold piece (*aureus*) did not weigh more than half its original value in Augustus' time, and silver coins contained as much as 95 per cent, if not 99 percent alloy additive. Even copper and bronze, now too expensive, were abandoned as alloy additive or alloy in favor of baser metals: tin, zinc, and lead. The cities and the Senate gave up issuing bronze coins, not for political reasons, but because such metals became worth more in weight than the official value of the coin.

First Diocletian and then Constantine were to bring about a vigorous recovery program for the precious-metal coinage. But inflation was to continue, so far as bronze money was concerned. The result was therefore a kind of monetary duality, analogous to that in Egypt under the Ptolemies, and which to some degree presaged (with metallic coinage) the contemporary system of exchange control (internal inflation, monopoly of gold for foreign trade).

Diocletian issued an *aureus* of weight intermediate between Augustus' and that of his immediate predecessors (5.45 grams, i.e., at the rate of 60 Roman *libra* of 327 grams). Constantine devalued it by one-fifth (4.55 grams, i.e., 72 per *libra*). This piece was called the *solidus,* i.e., the integral *aureus:* The French have derived the word *sou* from it. This gold *solidus* was never to be devalued and remained invariant in the Eastern Empire until the time of the Commeni emperors in the eleventh century. Its name in old French was "bezant" (Byzantine). This remarkable stability in a world which had abandoned gold coinage must have brought pride and glory to the Byzantines.

In the case of silver, Diocletian restored the *denarius* of the first century A.D. (3.41 grams, i.e., 96 per *libra*). But of the two metals, gold predominated and was the official "nominal money."

But this "good money," struck in precious metal, was not in circulation to any appreciable extent. A single workshop coined the gold piece, and its issue was discontinued. This was certainly the reason why laws decreed that fines must be paid in weight of metal. This coinage served for foreign use (like the gold exchange standard of the years around 1928), and also for political ends: munificent gifts, or tribute made over to the barbarians to bribe them to refrain from attack. The coinage enjoyed only domestic circulation and disappeared into the hiding places of hoarders. To facilitate its use, Theodosius issued some coins of lower denomination called *triens,* worth one-third *solidus.* It had only a slight degree of success.

The basis of the money pool was in reality copper and bronze coins, constantly devalued, especially under Constantine, then again under Theodosius. It is true that there were occasional attempts at restoring the standard, marked by the issue of coins of higher standard, but they were hoarded and immediately disappeared (Gresham's Law).* Thus it was possible to write: "The monetary history of the fourth century is that of a series of devaluations, interrupted from time to time by attempts, usually unsuccessful, at deflation" (Piganiol).

Of all the subdivisions of the empire, Egypt was the most affected. She kept to the local *drachma,* theoretically equivalent to the *sestertius,* a bronze coin in which a little silver had formerly been added, and which had almost disappeared by the Later Empire. From A.D. 301 to 400, the value of the gold *solidus* went from 4,000 to 180 million Egyptian *drachmai!* It was a real case of "galloping consumption," entirely localized, however, in this country (perhaps to facilitate pillaging her of her exceptional wealth).

* "Bad money drives out good."—TRANSLATOR'S NOTE.

This crisis brought with it two main results: a rise in prices, and a return to barter economy. The first, a consequence of the increase in the amount of money in circulation, is an application of the quantitative theory of money. In Egypt, the price of the same measure of wheat, 6 *drachmai* in the first century A.D., rose to 200 in A.D. 276. The cost was 9,000 in 314, 78,000 in 334, and rose to more than 2 million shortly after 344. Although less spectacular, the rise in cost was no less evident in the rest of the empire.

Furthermore, as people avoided the use of this increasingly worthless coinage, there was some degree of reversion to a moneyless barter economy. Many taxes, indeed, were collected in kind; warehouses had to be built to store the goods, and to have them transported by the official mail service, with all the expense and confusion which that entailed. Soldiers and officials received at least a portion of their pay or salary in kind. On the large estates, autarchy enabled specie to be dispensed with. But it would be wrong to paint too gloomy a picture. Some recent work has proved that the monetary economy, while very unsettled in the third century, tended to recover its balance in the fourth, except in Egypt; and that it was to hold out until the end of the empire. Toward the end of the fourth century, the *adaeratio* was even restored—the possibility of collecting pay and salary in cash—and to permit use of old tariffs, the official price scales gave the relationships between commodities and money.

C. Crisis in Circulation and Exchange

The civil wars and regional insurrections, and the deep penetration of the barbarian armies all hindered the circulation of people and goods; they also brought brigandage and piracy. In A.D. 417, the Gallic poet Rutilius Namatianus reached Rome by sea, the overland routes being too dangerous. But soon the seaways themselves were no better because of raids by the Vandals, now established in Africa.

Credit fell to the very lowest level, with its corollary, the growth of usury. The Church Fathers denounced incessantly the scourge ("whirlpool") of usury, against which ecclesiastical and civil legislators fought with difficulty.

The balance of profits and payments remained in the red for commercial reasons with political factors added. The empire paid in gold for the luxury products which it continued to import from the Far East; and now it was paying off its barbarian mercenaries in gold and often turned over tribute to the barbarians themselves to buy peace, which was still less expensive than war.

Italy and Rome ceased to be the hub of commerce, which became decentralized and increasingly made use of the Rhine and Danube route to reach Constantinople, bypassing Italy altogether. Italian merchants disappeared, and even at Ravenna many Syrian merchants set up in business.

Nevertheless, the empire's balance of trade with the East improved noticeably in the sixth century. One of the most expensive imports, silk, which till this time came all the way from China or from Sassanid Persia, began to be cultivated in Syria from A.D. 552 onward, thanks to cocoons brought back by missionary monks. Also, a great effort was made to develop the export of luxury wares: the West, occupied by the barbarians, bought from the Eastern Empire fabrics (often imitations of the Persian), carpets, even capitals of marble columns which were transported already sculpted. Up till this time, purple was the prerogative of the imperial court, but it now began to be exported to the East.

D. Crisis in the Distribution of Wealth

The disparities of the Early Empire worsened. That between the East, always prosperous, and the declining West became more marked. We must add to this geographic contrast those internal disparities, especially in wealth. Apart from a few merchants, the middle class was in the process of disappearing, in the West at least; it had originally consisted of decurions, the municipal magistrates. These men had long since become impoverished by their acts of generosity and were now ruined by the fiscal system which had placed on their shoulders the responsibility of taxation. They avoided this crushing burden by all available means.

The larger fortunes, however, were in process of growth. Several families in Rome, shortly after A.D. 400, drew a revenue of 4,000 *librae* (1,310 kilograms) of gold per year, plus one-third of this in kind. They displayed unprecedented luxury. Several Antiocheia families had one to two thousand slaves. (Toward the end of the fourth century, St. Melania began her edifying life by freeing all of her 8,000 slaves simultaneously.) The concentration of landownership intensified. Lands were added to lands, privilege to privilege, and feudalism began to appear prior to the barbarian invasions. It has been said with reason that, at the moment of imperial collapse in the West, all Italy lay in the hands of the equivalent of the modern French "two hundred families," in the senatorial class.

In the face of such wealth, the poor were intensely wretched. Merging of the slave and the free peasantry classes was in progress: whilst the slaves were "settled," the colonists could see their own condition approaching that of serfdom. Despite several sporadic revolts, notably in Gaul (the Bagaudae) and in Africa (the Circumcellions), this evolutionary process, far from occurring in an atmosphere of class warfare, took place in a climate of humble submission. The *humiliores* yielded without resistance to the pressure of the *potentes* and even came to beg their protection, appealing to them (*commendatio*), since the state no longer exerted any hold there. The *potentes* extended their influence over whole villages (*patrocinia vicorum*). Only the imperial legislator, who felt the reins slipping out of his hands, attempted to combat this usurpation of power, but in the teeth of public opinion.

In the towns also, the wretchedness of the poor was marked. In Rome it was palliated by the *annona* distributions, which persisted for a long period. In Constantinople (*ca.* A.D. 400) St. John Chrysostom could say that half the population was on church relief.

Certain towns in the East were, however, flourishing. Antiocheia was a very beautiful town whose illumination at night enhanced her fame. Constantinople was a city of magnificent architecture. But in the West, towns were on the decline and some, both small and average sized, almost disappeared. Fiscal laws had a crushing effect on them: decurions, now bankrupt, did not offer, as they used to, beautiful works of art for public display. Only ramparts were built, and surrounding only a restricted area. Food supplies were costly, especially for those who only had devalued money at their disposal. Obstacles in the way of the circulation of commodities led to famine, such as occurred in Rome (A.D. 398) as the result of a revolt in Africa. On top of all that, the barbarians made surprise attacks, primarily on the towns, which they pillaged and burned, and there was no means of rebuilding them.

People gradually moved out from town to country. A genuine return to the land occurred, marked by land clearance. In this way the food-supply problem was solved, but it was the end of all ancient civilization founded on the city. "The estate is the nucleus of the feudal system, while the town was the birthplace of freedom." [1]

II. THE PLANNED ECONOMY

The imperial government sought a remedy for all these difficulties by means of the planned economy. It was the third experiment of its kind made in antiquity, this time spanning the Roman world and with objectives different from

[1] M. Weber, *Die sozialen Gründe des Untergangs der antiken Kultur* (1924) pp. 289 ff.

those of the preceding occasions; this confirms the observation that state planning can adapt to quite different kinds of problems. It was no longer a question of paternalism, the state in the role of universal provider, as in the Egypt of the pharaohs; nor of fiscal exploitation pure and simple, as under the Lagids. Also far removed from the ideas of that period would be the state-control trends of our epoch. In reality, neither Greeks nor Romans in antiquity ever had a hard-and-fast economic doctrine. They never professed the liberal dogma (which certainly does not date back further than the Physiocratic school). Intervention of cities and states in the economy had been frequent in all periods, more or less on a basis of expediency, and especially important wherever grain or food supplies were involved. But, aside from Egypt, these interventions had either affected a limited area only, or were short-term. Conversely, in the Later Empire the economy was planned without any fixed design in mind. There was no doctrinal direction of the economy; no anti-liberal thesis was upheld there. As for social disturbances, they hardly got beyond the level of angry gestures by authority against certain abuses of the rich. Crisis preceded regimentation and provoked it. State intervention had its origin in necessity, above all in the insatiable needs of the state: it needed an army, and therefore men, money, and supplies; it had to feed Rome and to defend authority against usurpation by the powerful. Necessity was the hallmark: it was "an economy of a state of seige." [2] But the vast extent of its urgent demands incited men to fraud and tax evasion; this led to a battle between the fraudulent and the legislator, who enacted a system of regulations more and more extensive and detailed. The state, moreover, did not limit itself to issuing orders; it also took direct action. Finally, it complemented its operations by means of the professional and corporate organization.

[2] F. Lot, *La fin du monde antique et le début du Moyen Age* (1927), p. 115.

A. Regulation of the Economy

Besides the question of Rome's food supplies, regulation affected all branches of the economy, especially production and trade.

The most important measures tended to bring wasteland under cultivation; such land was untaxed and consituted a besetting problem for the government. Attempts were made to attract farmers by promising them secure rights over the land they occupied. But more often compulsion was the preferred method; its chief application was *adjectio* (in Greek, *epibole*), which was to make the village (i.e., the other farmers) responsible for the tax due on the abandoned land. This was a system of collective responsibility with precedents in Ptolemaic Egypt, and which also conforms to the very principle of distributed taxation (*impôt de répartition*). Likewise, state lands which remained without voluntary farm labor were officially assigned to neighboring landowners.

In monetary affairs, ineffectual regulations were decreed to combat Gresham's Law and domestic speculation in the different kinds of money. It was forbidden to buy or sell coins: they had to be used for payment only. It was even forbidden to hoard them! It was forbidden to melt them down (to extract the small amount of silver alloyed with the bronze). The punishment for all these offenses was death. Controls were set up along roads and at ports, where the police searched traders and travelers. Of course, all these efforts were to no purpose.

Attempts were also made to combat the rise in prices. Many epigraphic finds have enabled a reconstruction to be made of the famous Edict of Prices, decreed by Diocletian in A.D. 301. It contained a table of maximum prices for thousands of articles, commodities, or services, with meticulous distinctions according to the quality of the item. Nothing like this had ever been done before: governments had been content to tax wheat, but not everything at the same time.

The penalties, here too, were terribly severe: death for anyone who sold too dear, even for one who bought too dear; death for hoarders who refused to sell and who concealed the possession of stock. Lactantius, an enemy of Diocletian, maintained that this led to a good deal of bloodshed. This has never been proved. It appears more probable that the edict was a complete failure, and it had to be withdrawn. A new attempt was made in 362, under Julian, perhaps restricted to Antiocheia. This, too, failed due to "force of circumstance," as was recognized nevertheless by one of his well-wishers, Ammianus Marcellinus.

Legislation was also continuously enacted against usury. In its final stage, under Justinian, it limited interest to 6 per cent per annum in civil affairs, 8 per cent in questions of trade (12 per cent for the maritime loan, *nauticum foenus*). Never before had the rates been set so low. Furthermore, compounding of loan interest (anatocism) was prohibited.

Foreign trade also was subjected to many controls. The laws forbade many types of export, whether abroad in general, or more specially to enemy or barbarian countries. These prohibitions applied primarily to what we should call "strategic products": iron, bronze, weapons, army equipment, and horses. They were then extended to cover food supplies (grain, wine, oil) reserved for a hungry empire; then later to cover gold, for mercantilist reasons, or just to limit the budget deficit. With the same objectives in mind, unauthorized importation of costly merchandise (e.g., silk) was forbidden. These various prohibitions, combined with a most stringent customs control, amounted to a kind of exchange control.

B. Direct State Intervention

The state sometimes acted more directly. It took part in production. The emperor owned vast territories, most of the mines, the workshops and organizations manufacturing silk, purple, silver and gold embroidery, and papyrus; even quarries and brickfields. Usually the labor force was slave or penitentiary: being condemned to forced labor was termed *ad metalla* (to the mines). People could even be condemned to work in the state spinning mills.

There were similar interventions in exchange. The state bought, sold, and requisitioned large amounts of commodities, and collected taxes in kind. It held many monopolies (e.g., manufacture, and even use, of purple). To allow the silk industry to keep itself supplied despite the war against Persia, who obstructed imports, Justinian had his agents buy supplies and sell them to the spinners. He even went so far as to redeem businesses that had been forced to shut down.

Lastly, the state intervened in distribution and consumption. The *annona* service and food distributions increased, a situation made worse by demagogues, and they continued to operate until the end of the Western Empire. Severus Alexander had bread distributed instead of wheat. To help the producers of Tripolitania, victims of slumps, Septimius Severus before him had likewise distributed oil. Aurelian added pig fat to the list. Besides these free handouts for the poor only, the state sold various foodstuffs at reduced prices to all consumers, regardless of wealth.

C. Professional and Corporate Organizations

In the usual way (*vide* 1940 in Europe), organization of the professions went hand in hand with state intervention and complemented it. The corporate system was formed in the third century and intensified in the fourth. A system of this kind is characterized first of all by the existence of corporations, comprising, profession by profession, both artisans and merchants and with spokesmen and a patrimony in common. But this feature alone would not suffice to define a corporative system: *corpora* or *collegia* of this kind were in existence from before the Roman Empire. More important here was the obligation which was henceforth imposed upon all who carried on a profession to be a member of the corporation, which was granted a monopoly. Another characteristic is the system of very detailed regulations. Each corporation had privileges, professional or otherwise (exemption from tax, from corvées, from municipal charges, for its members); but there were also obligations such as working for the state —a frequent requirement. The corporate society thus served as an intermediary; the state controlled it, but it in turn controlled the members, and this explains the growth of the system. This is what is called in France "state corporatism." Lastly, we can speak of a corporative system because the corporations extended over many professions. In the third century, corporations encompassed everything that involved Rome's food supply, from ship chandlers (*navicularii*) to bakers. In the following centuries, most professions were incorporated: even notaries, bankers, and actors. It was with difficulty that certain freedom-loving professions (lawyers, doctors) succeeded in escaping incorporation. There is one thing that should be said about these groupings; they were always limited to a local area. There was a guild of butchers of Rome, another of Constantinople, and others of various towns; but none common to the whole empire, like the professional federations of our own times.

Another means of coercion was instituted in the course of the fourth century: compulsory labor supplemented by the hereditary profession. It was very rare that anyone was officially forced to take up a given craft or profession, but those who exercised any trade regarded as indispensable (in food, for example) were tied to it permanently, or could only leave it if they provided a replacement and gave up their goods to him. Aurelian had already compared leaving a profession with desertion. The next procedure was to "freeze" a man's own property, in order to hold him: Valentinian in A.D. 365 revoked the property alienations made by the ship chandlers.

A *curialis* (member of the municipal Senate, responsible for levying taxes) could not give up his property without authorization. Then it was decided that anyone who acquired such property had to carry on the trade, like a trust which was entailed by it. Some of the laws, which increased in number around A.D. 325, applied this principle to goods inherited, which resulted in a true system of hereditary castes. But although this system was introduced as a patrimonial matter, it went beyond paternal inheritance. It could happen that a son had to succeed his father in a profession, quite independently of transfer of property. Even a marriage could sometimes have, as corollary, compulsory entry to a profession: he who married a baker's daughter had to become a baker! These rules could also lead to embarrassing situations. If a ship-outfitter inherited from a baker, what must he do? Preference was given in this case to the ship chandler's profession. In other cases, one would have to carry on both trades. What happened if a professional man died without heirs? It was decided that his property should go to the *consortium,* i.e., to the corporation or guild. But all these problems increased in number, specious argumentation about them was on the increase, and regulations became more and more detailed to resolve the difficulties. The system had been created for food-supply trades, but it was not long in extending its application. In A.D. 313, Constantine forced every soldier's son to be a soldier, unless unfit for service, in which case he had to become a *curialis* (member of the municipal assembly). In 331, he empowered officials to make their children their successors; but later, this hereditary system, far from being a privilege, became an obligation for many officials, whose sons had to choose between service in the administration or the army. Similarly colonists, farmers of the large estates, were tied to the land on a permanent and hereditary basis. The position of *curialis,* not exactly a profession, likewise became hereditary, with a view to ensuring regular tax returns. In short, the tendency was to extend this system to every job which was both unpleasant and indispensable in order to keep up recruitment.

CONCLUDING REMARKS

Did the planned economy ruin the empire? Some have said that it did,[3] while others have thought the contrary—that the state had to interfere and did so effectively.[4] One thing is certain—crisis preceded regimentation, which inclines one to favor the second opinion. Nevertheless, this system of regulation would have gained by being more humane. Coercion was preferred to more gentle methods of directing the economy. Men were trapped in the situation where chance had placed them. Perhaps some success of a purely economic nature was obtained in this way, but on the human and social planes the system was a failure. State intervention and a crushing fiscal policy made the whole empire groan under the yoke; more than once, both poor men and rich prayed that the barbarians would deliver them from it. In A.D. 378, the Balkan miners went over en masse to the Visigoth invaders, and just prior to A.D. 500 the priest Salvian expressed the universal resignation to barbarian domination.

At least since Montesquieu, the source of the Roman decline has been sought; in the eyes of modern historians, it lay in the economic and financial sphere. One fact is vital to note: the Western Empire collapsed in the fifth century, whereas the Eastern resisted successfully; this was because the West was poor. Her budget has been estimated at one third of that of the Eastern Empire, which could keep up her army and sometimes use tribute to buy peace from the more turbulent of her neighbors. Disasters befell her in her turn, however, during the seventh century; but she was already bankrupt by the sixth. The glorious reign of Justinian (527–

[3] H. M. R. Leopold, *De Spiegel van het Verleden* (1918).

[4] F. M. Heichelheim, "Welthistorische Geschichtspunkte" in *Schmollers Jahrbuch*, LVI, 994 ff.; LVII, 1034 ff.

65) was in some respects just one long blunder, because he used up the resources of the East in laborious and ephemeral reconquests, not to mention his costly buildings (Sancta Sophia). Yet Constantinople found in the traditional prosperity of the eastern regions the strength to outlive, somehow or other, the ruin of the Roman Empire proper by almost a thousand years.

Conclusion

The barbarian invasions provoked a twofold break: first, with the economic regime of the Later Empire. The state-controlled economy disappeared, and state intervention suffered an almost identical fate. All those problems which arose in such serious form were forcibly simplified. But there was a second break: with the economy of the ancient world. The economy retrogressed, if not to the point of departure, at least by several centuries.

But when and to what extent did the economy of antiquity draw to its close? Current opinion assigns the major role to the invasions, which caused a decline in trade and a complete break between the ancient and the Frankish economies. The German historian Dopsch at the beginning of the century spoke out against this view, stating that the Mediterranean remained, at least over the whole Merovingian period, the axis of trade and that all eyes were still turned toward Constantinople, capital of the empire and much-admired metropolis of trade and civilization. His view (not without important differences) was revived with some force by Henri Pirenne around 1930, in his book *Mahomet et Charlemagne*. The Merovingians, in his opinion, merely carried on Roman economic activity in much restricted form. It was only the Arab conquest which cut off Gaul from the eastern world and so prevented navigation of the Mediterranean: "The sea, which till then had been the centre of Christendom, became its frontier." This event brought with it a series of consequences: the ruin of trade; predominance of agriculture in a closed regional economy; and, after some centuries of stagnation, a new departure for western economy, but now toward northern Europe, turning its back on the Mediterranean.

It is not our task in this book to judge whether the role played by the Arabs was destructive or whether, as M. Lombard stated in 1947, it was promotive. Our problem is simply to understand whether the Frankish economy was a prolongation of that of antiquity, or had characteristics which were diametrically different. The difference between commerce in antiquity and in the Merovingian period could perhaps be explained, at least partially, by a shift in viewpoint. The economy of the Roman Empire is seen from Rome and from the borders of the Mediterranean, in the light of Latin and Greek sources. But when we consider the period of the Franks, we view it from the banks of the Seine and the Loire, using local texts. Now, from before the invasions, Gaul was nowhere near being the hub of commerce. This remark may help to put in its proper perspective the decadence that is claimed. That decadence, however, was both obvious and advanced.

Decadence affected, first of all, the commodities traded and the amounts handled. Certainly, up to the time of the Arab conquest, oil continued to be imported from Africa and papyrus from Egypt. But otherwise long-distance transportation involved scarcely anything but luxury items such as jewels, spices, fabrics, and works of art; this constitutes a return to a time several centuries earlier. And when anyone invokes in support of the theses of Dopsch or Pirenne the preservation of this kind of importation, the argument is null and void, because luxury trade is both very primitive and yet, so to speak, perpetual because it never disappears. On the other hand, foodstuffs were hardly shipped at all any more; and sooner than have them brought to their residences, kings preferred to go and consume them in situ, which involved continual traveling. Trade was now just an occasional affair: it was only when a production surplus was in danger of deterioration, or when all stores had been used up after poor harvests, that people resigned themselves to buying and selling: "Sale and purchase . . . were the expedients to which men resorted when necessity enforced them." [1]

Decadence also affected the techniques of trade. The sedentary commerce of the towns almost disappeared, and its place was taken by the market and soon by the fair. There were only Syrian traders up to the beginning of the eighth century, then some Jews, or "Frisian" boatmen. The profession was not well thought of. From now on, a sale was made directly between producer and consumer at the local level, or sometimes farther afield by permanent agents of monasteries, negotiating on their behalf. Gold disappeared, drained towards the East by the deficit in the balance of payments, and Charlemagne drew the appropriate inference when he set up a system of silver monometallism. Barter economy increased enormously, wine being used as nominal money, especially in the region around Paris. Rents and taxes were paid in kind; agents of the government received lands by way of remuneration. Lastly, it was no longer possible to speak of banks or credit, and Charlemagne could ban every kind of interest loan.

Trade fell into the background of economic life. "Land was the sole source of subsistence." [2] The large estate, now so widespread, tended to autarchy, to closed economy. There were groups of artisans to be found carrying on all trades, all forms of husbandry, even that of the vine in regions little suited to it; or, if it was genuinely impossible, the big landowner procurred himself an estate further south on which to produce his wine. Thus, despite the survival of some guilds

[1] H. Pirenne *et al., La civilisation occidentale au Moyen Age du XIe au milieu du XVe siècles* (*Histoire Générale*, gen. ed., G. Glotz [Paris, s.d.]), III, 14. See also the equivalent reference: H. Pirenne, *Histoire économique de l'Occident Médiéval* (Bruges, 1951), p. 165.

[2] *Ibid.*, p. 12(=*ibid.* p. 162).

in southern Gaul and in Italy, everywhere else the towns became smaller and only served as places for bishops to reside, or as a place of refuge behind town walls.

Generally speaking, in the Merovingian period the economy was "adrift"; "the rot had set in." [3] The ancient world appeared to continue on, but this was merely a facade behind which virtually nothing took place. After the short-lived, or pseudo-renaissance of the Carolingian period, and after renewed invasion, a renaissance began to be visible from the end of the ninth century or by the tenth. But we are no longer dealing with the economy of antiquity: it was the birth of the European economy.

[3] R. Latouche, "Les origines de l'economie occidentale," in *L'evolution de l'humanite,* XLIII, 163–64.

Chronology

Cautionary note: No date is certain before the ninth century B.C. For example, the beginning of the first Babylonian dynasty is set by some authorities at 2169 B.C. and by others at 2105, 2049, or 1813 B.C. The internal chronology of this dynasty is well established, but the uncertainty about its beginning date means that the reign of Hammurabi varies, according to the estimates in question, from 2067–2025 B.C. to 1711–1669 B.C. We shall adopt the latter dates, regarded by present-day specialists as the more probable, but we shall do so without offering any guarantee of accuracy. Consult M. J. Delorme's books *Les grandes dates de l'Antiquité* ("Que sais-je?" Series, [Paris, 1962]), and *Les grandes dates de Moyen Age* ("Que sais-je?" Series, [Paris, 1963]).

I. The Ancient World to Alexander (to 330 B.C.)

WEST	GREEK WORLD	ASIA MINOR	SYRIA-PALESTINE	EGYPT	MESOPOTAMIA	IRAN
				3d millenium: Old Kingdom [capital city: Memphis]	3d millennium: predominance of the Sumerians [Ur]	
				Ca. 2700 or 2500 (?) apogee: 4th Dynasty [Pyramids]		
					The Akkadians [Semites] first appear	
			Before 2000: Byblos in communication with Egypt			
				Ca. 2000 or 1900: Middle Kingdom begins [capital city: Thebes] apogee: 12th Dynasty		
					Akkadians unify south	
					1813: start of 1st Babylonian dynasty	
		1st Hittite Empire				

				Hammurabi 1711-1669
			Hyksos invasion (prior to 1500)	
Apogee of Cretan civilization [~1500]			New Empire begins [capital city: Thebes]	Kassite invasion [*ca.* 1500 ?]
		Conquered by Egypt .... then by the Hittites	18th Dynasty	
	15th to 13th cent. } 2d Hittite Empire	15th and 14th cent. } invention of alphabets at Ugarit		
			Ca. 1400: traditional date of the Exodus [Moses]	
14th and 13th cent. } Mycenaean civilization	13th century: entente between Hittites and Egypt	Hebrews settle	Entente with the Hittites 19th Dynasty (Ramses II)	13th to 11th cent. } Assyrian conquests
2d half of 13th century legendary date of Trojan War	*Ca.* 1230: Hittites destroyed by the "Sea Peoples."	*Ca.* 1200: Philistines settle		

WEST	GREEK WORLD	ASIA MINOR	SYRIA-PALESTINE	EGYPT	MESOPOTAMIA	IRAN
	12th century: Dorian invasion		11th century: Samuel Saul, king of Israel	End of 12th century: invasion (repulsed) of the "Sea Peoples." Onset of decline	11th century: Assyrian withdrawal	
Around 1000: 1st Iron Age in Italy. Villanovan civilization	Obscure, confused period	Phrygian Kingdom	Tyre and Sidon powerful. David reigns in 1000	Partition 21st to 25th dynasties		
			Solomon (970–935) 939: schism (kingdoms of Israel and of Judah)			
814: legendary date of founding of Carthage						
Ca. 800: Etruscans in Tuscany	The Greeks established on both coasts of the Aegean Sea. Homeric poems composed					
	8th and 7th cent. } colonial development				8th century: Assyrian Empire	Kingdom of the Medes
754 (or 753): legendary date of foundation of Rome						
750: foundation of Cumae. First colony of Magna Graecia						

733: Syracuse founded					
			722: Sargon II takes over Samaria. Kingdom of Israel ends		Sargon II
708: Tarentum founded					
					7th century: Sennacherib Esarhaddon Ashurbanipal
				671–63: conquered by Assyrians	
				663: the 26th Dynasty liberates and reunifies the country [capital: Sais]. Psammetichus	
		7th century: kingdom of Lydia [Gyges]			
	621: Draco at Athens				
616: Tarquin the Elder is king at Rome					612: Nineveh destroyed by Medes and Chaldeans. Assyrian kingdom ends
Ca. 600: Massilia founded	594 (or 592): Solon, archon of Athens		588 (or 586): Jerusalem captured by Nebuchadnezzar		605 to 562: Nebuchadnezzar

WEST	GREEK WORLD	ASIA MINOR	SYRIA-PALESTINE	EGYPT	MESOPOTAMIA	IRAN
6th century: apogee of Etruscans						
	560 to 510: tyranny of Peisistratus and his sons	560 to 546: Croesus, king of Lydia 546: Croesus conquered by Cyrus. Lydian kingdom ends		560: Greeks start a colony at Naukratis	533: Cyrus captures Babylon	559(?) to 530: Cyrus, king of Persia
525: Battle of Alalia (Greeks *vs.* Carthaginians and Etruscans)	....	....	....	525: Cambyses conquers Egypt		530 to 522: Cambyses
						522 to 486: Darius
510: Tarquinius Superbus driven out. Founding of Roman Republic (according to tradition)	510: end of tyranny in Athens					
	490: 1st Median War. Battle of Marathon					
				486: Egypt frees herself from Persian rule	....	486 to 465: Xerxes
480: Battle of Himera; Syracusans defeat Carthaginians	480: 2d Median War. Salamis					

474: Syracusans defeat Etruscans at Cumae						
	Age of Pericles (Parthenon)					
						465: Artaxerxes
449: at Rome; Law of XII Tables (according to tradition)						
	432 to 404 } Peloponnesian War					
390: Gauls capture Rome	404: capture of Athens			30th Dynasty		
367 to 344 } Dionysius the Younger, tyrant of Syracuse						
	359 to 336 } Philip II, king of Macedonia			343: Egypt is reconquered by Persians		
338: Romans complete conquest of Latium	338: Battle of Chaeronea; Philip completes conquest of Greece					
	336–323: Alexander the Great	334: Alexander victorious at the river Granicus	333: Alexander wins Battle of Issos	Egypt conquered by Alexander	331: Alexander is victor at Arbela	
						330: death of Darius III, succeeded by Alexander

II. Hellenistic Period (330 to 31 B.C.)

WEST	GREECE & MACEDONIA	EGYPT	ASIA MINOR	SYRIA-PALESTINE	IRAN & MESOPOTAMIA
Wars of Romans against Samnites			323: death of Alexander the Great		
			306: final partition of his empire		
Ca. 290: Romans complete conquest of central Italy		Lagid Dynasty Ptolemy I Soter (306–283)		Seleukid Dynasty	
				Seleukos (306–280)	
War against Tarentum, and against Pyrrhus, king of Epiros, ended in 266		Ptolemy II Philadelphus (283–246)		Antiochos I (280–262)	
				Antiochos II (262–247)	*Ca.* 250: Parthian Arsacids conquer Iran
1st Punic War (264–241)					
Conquest of Cisalpine Gaul		Ptolemy III Euergetes (246–221)		Antiochos III (the Great) (224–188)	
2d Punic War (218-201), capture of Syracuse (211), Battle of Zama (202)					
	Romans defeat the Macedonians at Cynoscephalae (197)				
			Romans defeat Antiochos III at Magnesia (190)		

Conquest of Spain	Romans defeat Macedonians at Pydna (167)			Revolt of the Hasmoneans	
	End of Macedonian kingdom			Judaean War	
3d Punic War (149–146)					
146: destruction of Carthage	146: destruction of Corinth. Greece a Roman province	12 Ptolemy kings from Euergetes to Cleopatra			
			Romans annex kingdom of Pergamum (134)		
			Province of Asia formed		Parthians conquer Mesopotamia and take Babylon (129)
Narbonne founded (118)					
War against Jugurtha (112–105)					
			War against Mithridates (88–63)		
				Pompey destroys Seleukid Empire (64)	
J. Caesar conquers Gaul (58–51)					Romans defeated by Parthians at Carrhae. Crassus killed (53)
	Battle of Pharsalus (48)				
J. Caesar assassinated (44)					
	Battle of Actium (31)	Death of Cleopatra. Romans conquer Egypt			

III. The Roman Empire (31 B.C. to the middle of the 3d century A.D.)

Augustus (ruler of the empire from the Battle of Actium to his death in 14 A.D.)
The Christian era begins in his reign

Tiberius (14 A.D. to 37 A.D.): death of Christ occurs in his reign
Caligula (37-41)
Claudius (41-54)
Nero (54-68)
Flavian dynasty: Vespasian (69-79)
Titus (79-81)
Domitian (81-96)
Dynasty of the Antonines:
Nerva (96-98)
Trajan (98-117); conquest of Dacia and Mesopotamian campaign against Parthians. Conquests completed
Hadrian (117-38)
Antoninus Pius (138-61)
Marcus Aurelius (161-80); start of defensive wars
Commodus (180-92)
Severan dynasty:
Septimius Severus (196-211)
Caracalla (211-17)
Heliogabalus
Severus Alexander (*d.* 235); during his reign, the Parthian Arsacids were replaced in Iran and Mesopotamia by the Persian Sassanids, who ruled till the Arab conquest
Confused period follows, with "military anarchy" (Gordianus, Valerian, Gallienus, Claudius II, Aurelian)

IV. Later Roman Empire (middle of 3d century to 565 A.D.)

Diocletian (284-305) and Maximian (tetrarchy)
Constantine (312-37)
Sons of Constantine, especially Constantius
Julian the Apostate (360–63)
Valentinian I and II, Valens, Gratian, Theodosius (*d.* 395)

Western Empire	Eastern Empire
Honorius (till 423); Rome sacked by Visigoths in his reign	Arcadius (*d.* 408)
Valentinian III (till 455)	Theodosius II (*d.* 450)
Ca. 450–51: Huns invade. In 455 Rome sacked by Vandals, who came via Africa	Marcianus
Majorianus (*ca.* 460)	Leo
	Zeno
Western Empire ends in 476	Anastasius
Clovis (*d.* 511)	Justinus
	Justinian (527–65)

Bibliography

Significant information on economic history is to be found in works on general history, especially in the following:

The Cambridge Ancient History. Edited by J. B. Bury, S. A. Cook, F. E. Adcock, and M. P. Charlenworth. 12 vols. Cambridge, 1928–39.

Collection Clio. Paris: Presses Universitaires de France.

Histoire générale. General editor, G. Glotz. Paris: Presses Universitaires de France. 10 volumes on antiquity.

Histoire générale des civilisations. General editor, Maurice Crouzet. Vols. 1 and 2. Paris, 1953 and 1954.

Only texts or papers that specialize in economic history will be cited here.

Ancient Economic History in General

Economic History Texts Specially Concerned with Antiquity

The basic text is F. M. Heichelheim, *Wirtschaftsgeschichte des Altertums,* 2 vols. (Leyden, 1938); 2d ed. translated into English by J. Stevens, *An Ancient Economic History, from the Palaeolithic Age to the Migrations of the Germanic, Slavic, and Arabic Nations* (Leyden, 1958 and 1964). (Volume 1 deals with the prehistoric period, Oriental civilizations (pp. 96–192), and the beginnings of Mediterranean civilization up to 560 B.C. (pp. 193–294); the end of the book is taken up by notes. Volume 2 deals with Classical Greek economics from 560–330 B.C. The Hellenistic period will be treated in volume 3.)

Brentano, L. *Das Wirtschaftsleben der antiken Welt*. Jena, 1929 (2d ed.; Hildesheim, 1961).

Petino, A. *Storia Economica: Il mondo antico*. Catania, 1961.

Toutain, J. *L'économie antique* ("L'évolution de l'humanité Series," Vol. 20). Paris, 1927. Translated by M. R. Dobie, *The Economic Life of the Ancient World*. London, 1930. (The main concern of this book is the economic geography of antiquity.)

General Texts on Economic History Partly Devoted to Antiquity

See primarily:

Imbert, J. *Histoire économique, des origines à 1789* (Thémis Series). Paris: 1965, pp. 9–107 (excellent bibliography).

Richardot, H. and Schnapper, B. *Histoire des faits économiques*. Paris, 1963, pp. 5–92 (Roman economy only).

See also:

Clough, J. B. *The Economic Development of Western Civilization*. New York, 1959.

Fanfani, A. *Storia Economica*. Vol. 1. Turin, 1961.

Kuczynski, J. *Allgemeine Wirtschaftsgeschichte, von der Urzeit bis zur sozialistischen Gesellschaft*. Berlin, 1951.

Maillet, J. *Histoire des faits économiques, des origines au* 20e *siècle*. Paris, 1952. (Only a few pages devoted to antiquity; pro-Marxist leanings.)

Piettre, A. *Les trois âges de l'économie*. Paris, 1955 (2d ed., 1964). (The three ages are: the economy subordinated to religion; the economy independent and predominant; and the economy in decline as a result of state control and socialism. Pp. 19–152 apply this thesis to the ancient world; anti-Marxist tendencies.)

Prada, V. Vazquez de. *De los origenes a la revolución industrial* (*Historia Economica Mundial,* Vol. 1). Madrid, 1961.

Economic History Texts Devoted to an Important Section of Ancient Economic History

Three basic texts are:

Frank, Tenney *et al. An Economic Survey of Ancient Rome.* 6th ed. 6 vols. Patterson, N. J., 1959.

Vol. 1 by T. Frank (to the end of the Roman republic).

Vol. 2 by A. C. Johnson (Roman Egypt to the reign of Diocletian).

Vol. 3 by R. G. Collingwood (Great Britain), J. J. Van Nostrand (Spain), V. M. Scramuzza (Sicily), and A. Grenier (Gaul).

Vol. 4 by R. M. Haywood (Roman Africa), F. M. Heichelheim (Syria), J. Larsen (Greece), and T. Broughton (Asia Minor).

Vol. 5 by T. Frank (Rome and Italy).

Vol. 6, Index.

(This work is especially valuable for the amount of information it contains and for the regional monographs.)

Rostovtzeff, M. *The Social and Economic History of the Hellenistic World.* 3 vols. Oxford, 1941. (Deals with the period from Alexander the Great to Christian times. Volume 1 deals mainly with the third century B.C.; volume 2 deals with the last two centuries, period of the Roman conquest; volume 3 consists of notes and some appendixes, chiefly about coinages; numerous annotated illustrations.)

———. *The Social and Economic History of the Roman Empire.* 2d ed., revised by Fraser. 2 vols. Oxford, 1957. (Deals solely with the first three centuries after the beginning of the Christian era. Historical map; many annotated illustrations.)

Of less importance but providing excellent syntheses:

Frank, Tenney. *An Economic History of Rome.* 1st ed. London, 1926 (rev ed.; New York, 1962). (Unfortunately does not go beyond the second century A.D.; specially recommended.)

Gunther, R. and Schrot, G. (eds.). *Sozialökonomische Verhaltnisse im alten Orient u. im klassischen Altertum.* Berlin, 1961.

Heichelheim, F. M. "Römische Sozial- u. Wirtschaftsgeschichte" in *Römisches Weltreich u. Christentum* (Historia Mundi, Vol. 4). Munich, 1956, pp. 397–488.

Salvioli, G. *Il capitalismo antico: Storia dell' economia romana.* Edited by G. Brindisi. Bari, 1929.

Selected Articles on Ancient Economic History

Norton, P. R. Coleman (ed). *Studies in Roman Economic and Social History in Honour of Allen Chester Johnson.* Princeton, 1952.

For the works of the new Czechoslovakian school, consult:

Polacek, V. *Wirtschaft u. Staat im Altertum zu neueren Forschungen aus der CSSR. Studien zur Papyrologie . . . Fr. Oertel . . . gewidmet.* Bonn, 1964, pp. 137–45.

On Method

Lévy, J.-P. "Quelques remarques en matière d'histoire économique de l'Antiquité," *Annales de l'Université de Paris* (Paris, 1959), pp. 193–211.

Petino, A. "Senso e problemi dell' economica antica," in *Economia e storia 6, Studi in onore di V. Franchini.* Milan, 1959, pp. 259–73.

Specific Questions Relating to the Period of Antiquity as a Whole

AGRICULTURE

Le domaine (*Recueils de la Société Jean Bodin,* Vol. 4). Brussels: Editions de la Librairie Encyclopédique, 1949.

Jacob, H. E. *Histoire du pain depuis 6000 ans.* Translated by M. Gabelle.

Savoy, E. *L'agriculture à travers les âges.* Vol. 2. Paris, 1935 (from Hammurabi to the end of the Roman Empire).

TECHNOLOGY

Callé, G. de la, Castagnol, E. M., and Contenu, G. *Les origines de la civilisation technique* (*Histoire générale des techniques,* ed. M. Daumas, Vol. 1). Paris, 1962.

Derry, T. K. and Williams, T. L. *A Short History of Technology.* Oxford, 1960.

Dictionnaire Archéologique des Techniques. 2 vols. Paris: Editions de l'Accueil 1963–64.

Drachmann, A. G. *The Mechanical Technology of Greek and Roman Antiquity.* Copenhagen, 1963.

Forbes, R. J. *Studies in Ancient Technology.* 2d ed.; 9 vols. Leyden, 1964.

Singer, C., Homyard, E. J., and Williams, T. L. *A History of Technology.* 5 vols. Oxford, 1954.

TRANSPORTATION

Hancar, F. *Das Pferd im prähistorischer u. früher historischer Zeit.* Vienna and Munich, 1955.

Lefebvre des Noëttes, G. *L'attelage, le cheval de selle à travers les âges. Contribution a l'histoire de l'esclavage.* 2 vols. Paris, 1931 (a notable monograph).

Rousseau, P. *Histoire des transports.* Paris, 1963.

HISTORY OF LABOR

Jaccard, P. *Histoire sociale du travail de l'Antiquité à nos jours.* Paris, 1960 (84 pages on the ancient world).

LeFranc, G. *Histoire du travail et des travailleurs.* Paris, 1957.

Nougier, L. R., Garelli, P., Sauneron, S., Bourriot, F., Remondon, R. *Préhistoire et Antiquité (Histoire générale du travail,* gen. ed. L. H. Parias, Vol. 1). Paris, 1962.

SLAVERY

Aymard, A. *L'esclavage dans les societés antiques: Proche-Orient, monde grec, monde romain.* Paris, 1957.

Etat et classes dans l'Antiquité esclavagiste. Structure. Evolution (Recherches internationales à la lumière du marxisme, Book 2). Paris, 1957 (collection of articles published in eastern Europe, translated into French).

Finley, M. I. (ed.). *Slavery in Classical Antiquity. Views and Controversies.* Cambridge, 1960 (collection of articles by various authors).

Westermann, W. L. *The Slave Systems of Greek and Roman Antiquity.* Philadelphia, 1955.

COMMERCE

Lemosse, M. *Le commerce antique jusqu' aux invasions arabes* (*Histoire du commerce,* ed. J. Lacour-Gayet, Vol. 2). Paris, 1950, pp. 1–188.

Samhaber, E., *Histoire du commerce*. Paris, 1963.

Sédillot, R. *Histoire des marchands et des marchés*. Paris, 1964.

Szlechter, M. E. *Le contrat de société en Babylonie, en Grèce et à Rome*. Paris, 1947.

La foire (*Recueils de la Société Jean Bodin,* Vol. 5). Brussels: Editions de la Librairie Encyclopédique, 1953.

MONEY

Babelon, E. *Traité des monnaires grecques et romaines*. Paris, 1901 (many illustrations).

Babelon, J. *La numismatique antique* ("Que sais-je?" Series, No. 168). Paris, 1945.

Gaettens, R. *Inflationen. Das Drama der Geldenwertungen vom Altertum bis zur Gegenwart*. Munich, 1955.

Incarnati, L. *Moneta e scambio nell' Antichità e nell' alto Medio Evo*. Rome, 1953.

Mickwitz, G. "Le problème de l'or dans le monde antique," *Annales d'Histoire Economique et Sociale* (Paris, 1934), pp. 235–47.

Segré, A. "Some Traits of Monetary Inflations in Antiquity and the Middle Ages," *Seminar,* 1 (1943), 20–31.

Stengers, J. "Essai d'une méthode d'évaluation des sommes d'argent exprimées en monnaies anciennes," *Revue Belge de Philologie et d'Histoire* (Brussels, 1941), pp. 574 ff.

TOWNS

La Ville. 2. Institutions économiques et sociales (Recueils de la Société Jean Bodin, Vol. 7). Brussels: Editions de la Librairie Encyclopédique, 1955.

ECONOMIC CRISES

Schrot, G. "Der Charakter der Wirtschaftskrise im Altertum," *Acta Antiqua Academiae Scientarium Hungaricae,* 7 (1959), 251–83.

SOCIAL PROBLEMS

Pöhlmann, R. von. *Geschichte der sozialen Frage u. des Sozialismus in der antiken Welt*. 2 vols. 1925.

Riedmatten, L. de. *Le problème social à travers l'histoire*. 2d ed. Versailles, 1957.

ECONOMIC DOCTRINES

Of the innumerable histories of economic theories, the one which devotes the most pages to the ancient world is:

Denis, H. *Histoire de la pensée économique* (Thémis Series). Paris, 1966, pp. 5–71.

SELECTED TEXTS:

Barieri, G. "Fonti per la storia della dottrine economiche," *Dall' Antichità alla prima Scolastica*. Milan, 1958 (the treatment of classical antiquity stops at p. 104; then comes the Gospel, pp. 105 ff., then the Church Fathers, pp. 140 ff.).

Tozzi, G. *Economisti greci e romani*. Milan, 1961.

BIBLIOGRAPHY FOR EACH CHAPTER

CHAPTER ONE: THE GRAECO-ORIENTAL WORLD BEFORE ALEXANDER

I. General Conditions and Primitive Form of Ancient Economic Life

Delvoye, C. *Que pouvons-nous entrevoir de la vie économique de la péninsule grecque à l'époque neolithique*. Mélanges Georges Smets, 1952, pp. 189–206.

Fanfani, A. *Poemi omerici ed economia antica*. 2d. ed. Milan, 1962.

———. "La vita economica dell' antica Grecia secondo l'Iliade," in *Economia e storia, 6, Studi in onore del V. Franchini*. Milan, 1959, 1: 24–53.

Finley, M. I. "The Mycenaean Tablets and Economic History," *Economic History Review*, 10 (1957), 128–41.

Renard, G. *Le travail dans la préhistoire*. Paris, 1927.

Thurnwald, R. *Economics in Primitive Communities*. Oxford, 1932.

II. Two Great Economic Powers: Egypt and Mesopotamia

Cardascia, G. *Les archives des Murašu, une famille d'hommes d'affaires babyloniens à l'époque perse (445–403* B.C.).

Paris, 1951 (noteworthy text which deals with the whole economic life of the period).

Dairaines, S. *Un socialisme d'Etat quinze siècles avant J. C.* Law thesis, Faculté de Droit de l'Université de Paris, 1933.

Dykmans. *Histoire économique et sociale de l'ancienne Egypte.* 3 vols. Paris, 1936–37 (ends with the Old Kingdom).

Lambert, M. "L'économie mésopotamienne au 3e millénaire av. J. C." Humanities thesis, Faculté des Lettres de l'Université de Paris, 1958.

Leemans, W. F. *Foreign Trade in the Old Babylonian Period as Revealed by Texts from Southern Mesopotamia.* Leyden, 1960.

———. *The Old Babylonian Merchant, His Business and His Social Position.* Leyden, 1950.

Resina, G. "Sumer e Akkad," *La vita economica.* Catania, 1958.

Saval' Eva, T. N. *Agrarnyi stroj Egipta v period Drevnego carštva.* Moscow, 1962, p. 292 (agrarian structures in Egypt at the period of the Old Kingdom).

Tiumeneff, A. I. *Gosudarstvennoje chozjajstvo drevnego Sumera* (*The Economy of the State in Ancient Sumer*). Moscow and Leningrad, 1956.

III. Maritime and Colonial Expansion of the Phoenicians and Greeks

Berard, J. *La colonisation grecque de l'Italie meridionale et de la Sicile dans l'Antiquité.* Paris, 1957.

Contenau, G. *La civilisation phénicienne.* Paris, 1926.

Dauvillier, J. "Le droit maritime phénicien," *Revue Internationale des Droits de l'Antiquité* 6 (1959), 33–63.

Picard, G. and Picard, C. C. *La vie quotidienne à Carthage au temps d'Hannibal.* Paris, 1958.

IV. The First Appearance of Money

Andreae, W. "Ursprung, Formen und Arten des Geldes," in *Schmollers Jahrbuch für Gesetzgebung, Verwaltung, und Volkswirtschaft.* Berlin, 1952, pp. 411–30.

Angell, N. *The Story of Money.* London, 1934.

Gerloff, W. *Die Entstehung des Geldes u. die Anfänge des Geldwesens*. 3d. ed. Frankfurt am Main, 1947.

Kian, G. R. "Introduction à l'histoire de la monnaie et histoire monétaire de la Perse, des origines à la fin de la période parthe." Law thesis, Faculté de Droit de l'Université de Paris, 1933.

Laum, B. *Heiliges Geld. Eine historische Untersuchung über den sakralen Ursprung des Geldes*. Tübingen, 1924 (origin of money in religion; highly debatable view).

———. *Über das Wesen des Münzgeldes*. 1929.

Schlumberger, D. *L'argent grec dans l'Empire Achéménide*. Paris, 1953.

Will, E. "De l'aspect éthique des origines grecques de la monnaie," *Revue Historique*, 212 (Paris, 1954), 209–31.

V. The Economy in Classical Greece

GENERAL TEXTS

Bolkesteine, H. *Economic Life in Greece's Golden Age*. 2d ed. Edited by E. J. Jonkers. Leyden, 1958.

Cavaignac, E. *L'économie grecque*. Paris, 1951 (much statistical data, but to be treated with considerable caution).

Gernet, L. "Comment caractériser l'économie de la Grèce antique?" *Annales* (1933), pp. 561–66.

Glotz, G. *Le travail dans la Grèce ancienne depuis la période homérique jusqu' à la conquête romaine. Histoire économique de la Grèce*. Paris, 1920.

Michel, H. *The Economics of Ancient Greece*. Cambridge, 1957.

Will, E. "Limites, possibilités et tâches de l'histoire économique et sociale du monde grec antique," *Etudes Archéologiques* (Paris: Ecole des Hautes Etudes, 1963), pp. 153–66.

———. "Trois quarts de siècle de recherches sur l'économie grecque antique," *Annales, Economies, Sociétés, Civilisations* 9 (1954), 7–23.

FINANCE

Andréadès, A. N. *Storia delle finanze greche dai tempi eroici fino all' inizio dell' étà greco-macedonia*. Padua, 1961.

COMMERCE

Villard, F. "La eéramique grecque de Marseille (*6e–4e siècles*). Essai d'histoire économique." Humanities thesis, Faculté des Lettres de l'Université de Paris, 1958.

BANKING

Garrani, G. *Una grande banca nell' antica Atene: la trapeza di Pasione*. 1951.

INDUSTRY

Cloché, P. "La vie publique et privée des anciens Grecs" (*Les classes, les mêtiers, le trafic,* Vol. 5). Paris, 1931, p. 127 (especially technology).

Guirand, P. *La main d'ouvre industrielle dans l'ancienne Grèce*. Paris, 1950.

Hopper, R. J. "The Mines and Miners of Ancient Athens," *Greece and Rome* 30 (1961), 138–51.

AGRICULTURE

Finley, M. I. *Studies in Land and Credit in Ancient Athens (500–200* B.C.). *The Horos Inscriptions*. New Brunswick, N.J., 1951.

Jardé, A. *Les céréales dans l'Antiquité grecque*. Paris, 1925.

SOCIAL PROBLEMS

Mossé, C. "Aspects sociaux et politiques de la cité grecque au IVe siècle." *La fin de la démocratie athenienne*. Paris, 1962.

Woodhouse, W. J. *Solon the Liberator. A Study of the Agrarial Problem in Attica of the VIIth Century*. London, 1938.

CHAPTER TWO: THE HELLENISTIC ERA

As a whole:

Cavaignac, E. *L' économie grecque*. Paris, 1951.

Heichelheim, F. M. *Wirtschaftliche Schwankungen der Zeit von Alexander bis Augustus*. Jena, 1930.

Rostovtzeff, M. *The Social and Economic History of the Hellenistic World*. 3 vols. Oxford, 1941.

I. The Hellenistic and Carthaginian World

A. The General Conditions of Hellenistic Economics

Bellinger, A. R. *Essays on the Coinage of Alexander the Great.*

New York, 1963.

Casson, L. "The Grain Trade in the Hellenistic World," *Transactions and Proceedings of the American Philological Association* (1954) pp. 168–87.

Domarchi, J. "Aux origines de la décadence du monde antique: l'évolution économique des états hellénistiques," *Diogene* 2 (1954), 83–103.

Svencickaja, I. S. *Social'no-ekonomičeskoe osobennosti ellenistices-kikh gosudarsty* (*The Socioeconomic Peculiarities of the Hellenistic States*). Moscow, 1963.

B. The Decline of Greece

Valarché, J. *La Grèce de la décadence au point de vue économique et social.* Paris, 1941.

C. The Egyptian State-controlled Economy

See first:

Préaux, C. *L'économie royale des Lagides.* Brussels, 1939. This basic text is supplemented in *L'économie lagide, 1933–1958: Proceedings of the IXth Congress of Papyrology, Oslo, 1958.* Oslo, 1961, pp. 200–232.

PLANNED ECONOMY

Einaudi, L. *Greatness and Decline of Planned Economy in the Hellenistic World.* 1954.

AGRICULTURE

Bonneau, D. *La crue du Nil, divinité égyptienne, à travers mille ans d'histoire* (*332* B.C. *to* A.D. *641*). Paris, 1964.

Schnebel, M. *Die Landwirtschaft im hellenistischen Aegypten.* Munich, 1925.

MONEY AND THE BANK

Desvernois, J. "Banques et banquiers . . . sous les Ptolémeés," *Bulletin de la Société Archéol. Alexandrie* (1926), pp. 303–48.

Preisigke, F. *Girowesen im griechischen Aegypten, enthaltened Korngiro, Geldgiro, Girobanknotariat.* Strasbourg, 1910.

Segré, A. *Circolazione monetaria e prezzi nel mondo antico ed in particolare in Egitto.* Rome, 1922.

II. Roman Penetration into the Hellenistic Economy

On the Roman economy in general, see the works of Tenney Frank, cited above.

CURRENCIES AND FINANCES

Mommsen, T. *Geschichte des römischen Münzwesens, 1860–1862*. Berlin, 1860. Translated into French by the Duc de Blacas, *Histoire de la Monnaie romaine*. 4 vols. Paris, 1865, 1870, 1873, and 1875.

INDUSTRY

Louis, P. *Le travail dans le monde roman*. Paris, 1912.

Macqueron, J. *Le travail des hommes libres dans l'Antiquité romaine,* 2d ed. Aix-en-Provence, 1958 (legal in approach).

Martini, R. "Mercennarius," *Contributo allo studio dei rapporti di lavoro in diritto romano. Studi Senesi* (Siena) 68–69 (1956–57), 214–90 (rather legalistic).

Montevecchi, O. *I contratti di lavoro e di servizio nell'Egitto greco-romano e bizantino*. Milan, 1950.

Rémondon, R. In *Histoire générale du travail,* ed. L. H. Parias, Paris, 1962.

Robertis, F. M. de. *Lavoro e lavoratori nel mondo romano*. Bari, 1963.

A. Economic Antecedents in Italy up to the Third Century B.C.

Béraud, R. "L'évolution économique de Rome au début de la République." Law thesis, Faculté de Droit de l'Université de Grenoble, 1950.

Besnier, R. "L'état économique de Rome de 509 à 264 av. J. C.," *Revue Historique de Droit* 33 (1955), 195–226.

———. "L'état économique de Rome au temps des rois," *Revue Historique de Droit* 13 (1934), 405–63.

Bloch, R. *Les Etrusques* ("Que sais-je?" Series, No. 645). Paris, 1954.

Clerici, L. *Economia e finanze dei Romani, I*. Bologna, 1943 (to the end of the Samnite wars).

Curcio, G. *La primitiva civiltà latina agricola e il libro di M. Porcio Catone*. Florence, 1929 (highly technological).

Luzzatto, G. *Storia economica d'Italia. I. Antichità e Medio Evo.* Rome, 1949.

Pallottino, M. *La civilisation étrusque.* 2d ed. French translation by R. Bloch. Paris, 1955.

Papasogli, G. *L'agricoltura degli etruschi e dei romani.* Rome, 1942.

The first Roman coins:

Gamberini di Scarfea, C. *La monetazione di Roma prima e durante la Repubblica (dal V al I secolo A.C.).* 3d ed. Bologna, 1962.

Mattingly, H. "The First Age of the Roman Coinage," *Journal of Roman Studies,* 20 (1930), 19 ff.; 35 (1945), 65 ff.

Thomsen, R. *Early Roman Coinage.* 3 vols. Copenhagen, 1957.

B. The Integration of Rome in the Hellenistic Economy

Hatzfield, J. "Les trafiquants italiens dans l'Orient héllenistique." Humanities thesis, Université de Paris, 1919.

Mazzarino, S. "Les emprunts grecs dans le monde romain," *Actes du 1er Congrès de la Fédération Internationale des associations d'études classiques.* Paris, 1951, pp. 89–99.

For legal systems, see the numerous texts on Roman law and also:

Huvelin, P. *Etudes d'histoire du droit commercial romain.* Paris, 1929.

For businesses see:

Szlechter, M. E. *Le contrat de société en Babylonie, en Grèce et à Rome.* Paris, 1947.

For monetary systems and controversies about the dates of first appearance of the various coins, see primarily the basic (but controversial) works of H. Mattingly:

"The Date of the Roman Denarius." *Proc. of the British Academy* (1932), pp. 211–66 (this coin is here alleged not to have appeared prior to 187 B.C., but further excavations at Serra Orlando in Sicily have shown that it existed in 211; see R. Thomsen, *Early Roman Coinage,* 2: 358).

Roman Coins from the Earliest Times to the Fall of the Western Empire. London, 1960.

See also:

Belloni, G. *Le monete romane dell' étà repubblicana.* Milan, 1960 (detailed catalogue).

Breglia, L. "La prima fase della coniazone romana dell' argento," *Collezione di studi numismatici.* Rome, 1952 (asserts that the denarius dates back to 269 B.C.).

Carson, R. A. G. and Sutherland C. H. V. *Essays in Roman Coinage, presented to Harold Mattingly.* Oxford, 1956.

Hackens, T. "Le poids du denier romain vers la fin de la République," *Revue Belge de Numismatique,* 108 (1962), 29–47.

LeRoy, M. "Les étapes de la réduction du poids des monnaies de bronze de la République romaine," *Congrès International de Numismatique.* Paris, 1957, 2: 181–91.

Nicolet, G. "A Rome pendant la seconde guerre punique: techniques financières et manipulations monétaires," *Annales, Economies, Sociétés, Civilisations,* 18(1963) 417–37.

Piganiol, A. Reviews in *Revue Historique* 181 (1937) 44–46; 191 (1941) 292–95.

Pink, K. Reviews of "*The Triumviri Monetales* and *The Structure of the Coinage of the Roman Republic.*" *Journal of Roman Studies* (1953), pp. 193 ff.

Santini, A. "Ancora intorno alla data del primo denaro, 268 B.C. or 187 B.C.?" *Rivista Italiani di Numismatica,* 5 (1948), 84 ff.

Sydenham, E. A. *The Coinage of the Roman Republic.* London, 1952.

C. Exploitation of Conquest

On the tributes imposed on Sicily, see:

Carcopino, J. *La loi de Hiéron et les Romains.* Paris, 1919.

On the revenues and expenses of the state in 293 and 167 B.C., see the misleadingly entitled work:

Knapowski, R. *Der Staatschaushalt der römischen Republik.* Frankfurt-am-Main, 1961.

On the systematic control of viticulture:

Aymard, A. "Les capitalistes romains et la viticulture italienne," *Annales, Economies, Sociétés, Civilisations* 2 (1947), 257–65.

Bellini, L. "La viticoltura nella politica economica di Roma repubblicana," *Accademia Nazionale dei Lincei, Rendiconti della Classe di Scienze morali, storiche e filologiche* 2 (Ser. 8; 1947) 387–432.

D. The Repercussions in Italy

Krenkel, W. "Währungen, Preise u. Löhne in Rom," *Das Altertum* 7 (1961), 167–68.

Maroti, E. "Zur Frage der Warenproduktion in Catos de Agriculture," *Acta Antiqua Acad. Scient. Hungaricae* 11 (1963), 215–34.

THE LATIFUNDIA

Kuziscin, V. I. "O latifundjakh vo II veke do n.e. O tolkovanii 7-j gl. I knigi 'Graždanskikh vojn' Appiana" (Latifundia prior to the 2d century B.C. The interpretation of I,7 of Appian's "Civil Wars"), *Vestnik Drevnej Istorii,* 71 (1960), 46–60.

Salomon, P. *Essai sur les structures agraires de l'Italie centrale au IIe siècle av. J. C.* (Travaux et Recherches de la Faculté de Droit et des Sciences Economiques de Paris, Série Sciences Historiques, No. 3) Paris, 1964, pp. 1–68.

Tibiletti, G. "Lo sviluppo del latifondo in Italia dall' epoca graccana al principio dell' Impero" *(Relazioni del X° Congresso Internazionale di Scienze Storiche*). Florence, 1955, 2: 235–92.

———. "Ricerche di storia agraria romana," in *Athenaeum,* from 1948.

SOCIAL PROBLEMS

Bruwaene, M. van den. *Les origines et la formation (La société romaine,* Vol. 1.) Brussels, 1954.

Etat et classes dans l'Antiquité esclavagiste. Structure. Evolution. Recherches internationales à la lumière du marxisme, Book 2. Paris, 1957.

Hill, A. *The Roman Middle Class in the Republican Period.* Oxford, 1952 (deals mainly with the knights).

Lapicki, B. *Poglady Prawne Niewolników I Proletariuszy Rzymskich (Juridicial Views about Roman Slaves and Prole-*

taires).* Lodz, 1955 (this book has a summary in French). An abridged version in French will be found in:
Studi in onore di V. Arangio-Ruiz. Naples, 1953, 1: 245–71.

SUMPTUARY LAWS

Giraudias, E. Law thesis, Faculté de Droit de l'Université de Poitiers, 1910.

Chapter Three: The Early Roman Empire

For the overall economic life of this period, see the following monographs in addition to the general works by Rostovtzeff and Frank already cited:

Biraghi, G. "Il problema economico del regno di Nerva," *La Parola del Passato,* 19 (1951), 257–73.

Laet, S. J. de. *Aspects de la vie sociale et économique sous Auguste et Tibère*. Brussels, 1942.

MONEY (besides Mommsen):

Bolin, S. *State and Currency in the Roman Empire to 300* A.D. Stockholm, 1958.

Göbl, R. *Einführung in der Münzprägung der römischen Kaiserzeit*. Vienna, 1957.

Grant, M. *Roman Imperial Money*. London and Paris, 1954.

Mattingly, H., Sutherland, C. H. V., Carson, R. A. G., and Sydenham, E. A. *The Roman Imperial Coinage*. 9 vols. London, 1923–49.

Sutherland, C. H. V. *Coinage in Roman Imperial Policy*. London, 1951.

The special coinage of Egypt:

Milne, J. G. "Roman Coinage in Egypt in Relation to the Native Economy," *Aegyptus* 32 (1952), 143–51.

West, L. C. and Johnson, A. C. *Currency in Roman and Byzantine Egypt*. Princeton, N. J., 1944.

On devaluations (besides Gaettens):

* *Proletarii* were Roman citizens without military equipment or secure income, not the proletariat of modern socialist literature. Prof. Lévy's word is "prolétaires," by which he translated "Proletariuszy," and it is presumed he refers to the Roman, not the modern usage.—Translator's Note

Frank, T. "The Financial Crisis of 33 A.D.," *American Journal of Philology,* 56 (1935), 336–41.

Guey, J. "L' aloi du denier romain de 177 à 211 av. J. C., *Revue Numismatique* (1962), pp. 73–140.

———. "Le titre du denier romain sous l' empereur Commode," *Bulletin de la Société Française de Numismatique* 4 (1962), 137 ff.

Laet, S. J. de. *Une dévaluation dans l' Antiquité: la réforme monetaire de 64.* Brussels, 1942.

Pekáry, T. "Studien zur römischen Währungs- u. Finanzgeschichte von 161 bis 235 n. Chr.," *Historia,* 8 (1959), 443–89.

I. The Economic Apogee

A. Commercial Expansion

Charlesworth, M. P. *Trade-Routes and Commerce of the Roman Empire.* 2d ed. Hildesheim, 1961.

Majewski, K. "Récentes découvertes d' importations romaines en Pologne," *Annales, Economies, Sociétés, Civilisations* 15 (1960), 314–19.

Schwartz, J. "L' empire romain, l' Egypte et le commerce oriental," *Annales, Economies, Sociétés, Civilisations* 15 (1960) 18–44.

Warmington. *The Commerce between the Roman Empire and India.* Cambridge, 1928.

Special questions:

Demougeot, E. "Le chameau et l' Afrique du Nord romaine," *Annales, Economies, Sociétés, Civilisations* 15 (1960) 209 ff.

Gaudemet, J. "L' empire romain a-t-il connu les foires?" (*Recueil Société Jean Bodin,* Vol. 5) Brussels, 1953, pp. 25–42 (concludes it did not).

B. Progress of Agriculture

Camps-Fabrer, H. *L' olivier et l' huile dans l' Afrique romaine.* Algiers, 1953.

Fanfani, A. "Columella precursore de fisiocrati?" in *Economia e storia, 6, Studi in onore del V. Franchini,* Vol. 1. Milan, 1959, pp. 5 ff.

Kolendo, J. "La moissoneuse antique: son emploi en Gaule romaine," *Annales, Economies, Sociétés, Civilisations* 15 (1960), 1099–1114.

Parain, C. "Le problème de la diffusion réelle des progrès techniques dans l' agriculture romaine," in *Sozialökonomishe Verhältnisse im alten Orient und im klassischen Altertum*. Berlin, 1961, pp. 228–36.

Sirago, V. A. *L'Italia agraria sotto Trajano*. Louvain, 1958.

C. Industry

Davies, O. *Roman Mines in Europa*. Oxford, 1935.

Jones, A. H. M. "The Cloth Industry under the Roman Empire," *Economic History Review* 13 (1960), 183–92.

II. Imbalances

A. Imbalance between Production and Consumption

Berchem, D. van. *Les distributions de blé et d'argent à la Plèbe romaine sous l' Empire*. Geneva, 1939.

The size of the population of Rome is much in dispute. The lowest estimate is that of F. Lot. "Rome et sa population à la fin du 3e siècle de notre ère," *Annales d' Histoire Sociale* 2 (1945), 29–38 (the population of Rome is stated here not to have exceeded 220,000). Among the better known of opposing theories, see:

Carcopino, J. *La vie quotidienne à Rome à l' apogée de l' Empire*. Paris, 1939, pp. 30 ff. (estimates one or one-and-a-half million inhabitants).

Hammond. "Economic Stagnation in the Early Roman Empire," *Journal of Economic History* 6 (1946), 63–90.

B. Geographical Imbalances

See primarily *An Economic Survey of Ancient Rome* under general editorship of Tenney Frank, previously cited.

Day, J. *An Economic History of Athens under Roman Domination*. New York, 1942.

Duval, P. M. *La vie quotidienne en Gaule sous la paix romaine*. Paris, 1952.

Gansbeke, P. van. "La voie commerciale de la Bretagne au Rhin à l' époque romaine," *Revue Belge de Philologie et d' Histoire* 35 (1957), 746–62.

Harmand, L. *L'Occident romain: Gaule, Espagne, Afrique du Nord (31* B.C. *to 235* A.D.). Paris, 1960.

Johnson, A. C. *Egypt and the Roman Empire*. Ann Arbor, Mich., 1951.

Kahrstedt, U. *Das wirtschaftliche Gesicht Griechenlands in der Kaiserzeit*. Kleinstadt and Bern, 1954.

———. *Die wirtschaftliche Lage Grossgriechenlands in der Kaiserzeit*. Wiesbaden, 1960.

Loane, H. Jefferson. "Industry and Commerce of the City of Rome (− 50 + 200)," *Johns Hopkins University Studies in Historical and Political Sciences* 56 (2), (1938), 165–323.

Martinez, J. M. Blazquez. "La economia ganadera de la Espana antigua a la luz de las fuentes griegas y romanas," *Emerita*, 25 (1957), 159–84.

Picard, G. C. *La civilisation de l' Afrique romaine*. Paris, 1959.

III. Internal Transformations

A. Tendency toward business mergers

Bernard, N. "Fortune publique et fortune privée dans l' économie romaine (1st century B.C. to 1st century A.D.)." Law thesis, Faculté de Droit de l'Université de Grenoble, 1952.

Golovačev, I. F. "Melkoe e srednee zemlevladenie v Rimskoj Afrike" (The small- and medium-scale landed proprietor in Roman Africa), *Vestnik Drevnej Istorii*, 85 (1963), 136–53.

Maroi, F. "Fattorie agricolo-militari ai confini dell' impere romano," *Atti del congresso internat. diritto romano, Verona, 1947*. Milan, 1953, 4: 149–64.

Préaux, C. "La stabilité de l' Egypte aux deux premiers siècles de notre ère," *Chronique d' Egypte*, 31 (1956), 311–31 (continuation of previous state-control practices).

B. Changes in the Status of Farm Laborers

Merlat, P. *Pline-le-jeune, propriétaire foncier, Hommages à Léon Hermann*. Brussels, 1960, pp. 522–40.

Chapter Four: The Later Roman Empire

GENERAL TEXTS

The Cambridge Economic History of Europe from the Decline of the Roman Empire. Edited by J. H. Clapham, E. Power, M. Postan, and J. Habakkuk. Cambridge, 1942——.

Jones, A. H. M. *The Later Roman Empire* (284–602). *A Social, Economic, and Administrative Survey.* 3 vols. Oxford, 1964 (see especially vol. 2, chaps. 19 to 21, pp. 712 ff. concerning cities, the country, and industry, trade, and transportation).

Mazzarino, S. *Aspetti sociali del quarto secolo. Richerche di storia tardo-romana.* Rome, 1951 (deals with various economic and social questions).

———.*L' impero romano* (*Trattato di storia romana,* eds. G. Gianelli and S. Mazzarino, Vol. 2). Rome, 1956.

Specially devoted to the 3d century A.D.:

Calderini, A. *I Severi. La crisi del impero nel III secolo.* Bologna, 1949.

Oertel, F. "The Economic Life of the Empire," in *The Cambridge Ancient History.* Cambridge, 1939, 12: 232–81.

Walser, G. and Pekáry, T. *Die Krise des römischen Reiches. Bericht über die Forschungen zur Geschichte des 3. Jahrhunderts (193–284 n. Chr.) von 1939 bis 1959.* Berlin, 1962.

EGYPT

Johnson, A. C. and West, L. C. *Byzantine Egypt* (Economic Studies, Princeton University Studies on Papyrology). Princeton, N.J., 1949.

Byzantine economic history, in particular:

Vasiliev, A. A. *Justin the First.* 1950 (one chapter on economic history).

I. The Economic Crisis

Alföldi, A. "La grande crise du 4e siècle," in *L' Antiquité Classique.* Brussels, 1938, 7: 5–18 (excellent summary).

Fanfani, A. *Storia economica, Dalla crise dell' Impero romano al principio del secolo,* Vol. 18. Milan, 1941 (see the beginning portion of book).

Rémondon, R. *La crise de l' Empire romain, de Marc-Aurèle à Anastase.* Paris, 1964.

Ruggini, L. *Economia e società nell' Italia Annonaria. Rapporti fra agricoltura e commercio dal IV al VI secolo d.C.* Milan, 1961.

A. Crisis in Agricultural Production

Hannestad, K. *L' évolution des ressources agricoles de l' Italie du 4e au 6e siècle de notre ère.* Copenhagen, 1962.

Lemerle, P. "Esquisse pour une histoire agraire de Byzance: les sources et les problèmes," *Revue Historique,* 219 (1958), 32–74, 254–84; 220 (1958), 43–94.

Robertis, F. M. de. "La crisi del III secolo e l' avvio alla represa agricola in Italia," in *Studi di Storia medievale e moderna in onore di Ettore Rota.* Rome, 1954.

Rouillard, G. *La vie rurale dans l' Empire byzantin.* Paris, 1953.

The demographic question:

Boak, A. E. R. *Manpower Shortage and the Fall of the Roman Empire in the West.* Ann Arbor, Mich., 1955.

The large estates:

Ostrogorsky, G. "Le grand domaine de l' Empire byzantin," in *Recueils de la Société Jean Bodin,* Vol. 4. Brussels, 1949.

Special questions:

Diligenskij, G. G. *Severnaja Afrika v IV-V vekakh* (*North Africa in the 4th and 5th Centuries*). Moscow, 1961, pp. 113–48 (colonization, slavery, landed property, etc.).

Malafosse, J. de. "Le droit agraire au Bas Empire et dans l' Empire de l' Orient," *Rivista di Diritto Agrario,* 1 (1955), 35–73.

Schtajerman, E. M. *Die Krise der Sklavenhalterordnung im Western des römischen Reiches.* Translated by W. Seyfarth. Berlin, 1964.

B. Monetary Crisis

Cipolla, C. M. *Money, Prices, and Civilization in the Mediter-*

ranean World. Princeton, 1956 (fifth to seventeenth centuries).

Giesecke, W. *Antikes Geldwesen*. Leipzig, 1938.

Grierson, P. "The 'Tablettes Albertini' and the Value of the Solidus in the Fifth and Sixth Century A.D.," *Journal of Roman Studies* 49 (1959), 73–80.

Jones, A. H. M. "The Origin and Early History of the Follis," *Journal of Roman Studies* 49 (1959), 34–38.

Le Gentilhomme, P. "Variations du titre de la Antoninianus," *Revue Numismatique* 4 (1962), 141–66.

Mickwitz, G. *Geld u. Wirtschaft im römischen Reich des vierten Jahrhundert*. Helsingfors and Leipzig, 1932.

———. "Die Systeme des römischen Silbergeldes im IVten Jahrhundert," *Soc. Scient. Finn., Comm. Hum. Litt.* 6 (1933), 2.

Mill, P. V. *et al. Late Roman Bronze Coinage* A.D. *324–498*. London, 1960.

Piganiol, A. "Le problème de l'or au 4e siècle," *Annales d' Histoire Sociale* 1 (1945), 47–53.

Sutherland, C. H. V. "Denarius and Sestertius in Diocletian's Coinage Reform," *Journal of Roman Studies,* 51 (1961), 94–97.

C. Crisis in Circulation and Exchange

Ruggini, L. "Ebrei e orientali nell' Italia settentrionale fra il IV e il VI secolo d. Cr.," *Studia et Documenta Historiae et Iuris* 25 (1959), 186–308.

D. Crisis in the Distribution of Wealth

Leipoldt, J. *Der soziale Gedanke in der altchristlichen Kirche*. Leipzig, 1952.

For the pressure of the *potentes* and the *patrocinia* see:

Harmand, L. *Libanius, Discours sur les patronages. Texte traduit, annoté et commenté*. Paris, 1955.

II. The Planned Economy

Lambrechts, P. "Le problème du dirigisme d' Etat au 4e siècle,"

L' Antiquité classique 18 (1949), 109–26 (with bibliography).

Piganiol, A. "L' économie dirigée dans l' Empire romain au 4e siècle av. J. C.," *Scientia* 81 (1947), 95–100.

A. Regulation of the Economy

Dupont, C. *La réglementation economique dans les constitutions de Constantin*. Lille, 1963.

THE EDICT OF PRICES

The basic texts are:

Blümner, H. *Der Maximaltarif des Diokletian*. 2d ed. Berlin, 1958.

Bücher, K. "Die Diokletianische Taxenordnung vom Jahre 301," *Zeitschrift für die Staatswissenschaft* (1894).

Kent, R. G. "The Edict of Diocletian Fixing Maximum Prices," *University of Pennsylvania Law Review* (1920).

Frank, T. *An Economic Survey of Ancient Rome*. 6th ed. Paterson, N. J., 1959, 5: 305–422.

Supplementary works:

Bingen, J. "Nouveaux fragments delphiques de l'Edit du Maximum," *Bulletin de Correspondance Hellénique* 82 (1958), 602–9.

Caputo, G. and Goodchied, R. "Diocletian's Price-Edict at Ptolemaïs (Cyrenaica)," *Journal of Roman Studies* 45 (1955), 106–15.

Schönbauer, E. "Untersuchungen über die Rechtsentwickelung in der Kaiserzeit," *The Journal of Juristic Papyrology*, 9–10 (1955–56), 15–95.

Szilagyi, J. "Prices and Wages in the Western Provinces of the Roman Empire," *Acta Acad. Scient. Hungaricae* 11 (1963), 325–89.

B. Direct State Intervention

Chastagnol, A. *La préfecture urbaine à Rome sous le Bas Empire*. Paris, 1960, pp. 297 ff.

———. "Le ravitaillement de Rome en viande au 5e siècle," *Revue Historique* 210 (1953), 13–22.

Kohns, H. P. *Versorgungskrisen und Hungerrevolten im spätantiken Rom*. Bonn. 1961.

C. Professional and Corporate Organizations

The basic work on the corporative system remains that of J. P. Waltzing, *Etude historique sur les corporations professionnellas chez les Romains, depuis les origines jusqu' à la chute de l'Empire d'Occident*. 4 vols. Louvain, 1895–1902.

See also:

Robertis, F. M. de. *Il fenomeno associativo nel mondo romano. Dai collegi della Repubblica alle corporazioni del Basso Impero*. Naples, 1955.

COMPULSORY LABOR:

Nuyens, M. "La théorie des munera et l'obligation professionnelle au Bas Empire," *Revue Internationale des Droits de l'Antiquité* 5 (1958), 519–35.

CAUSES OF DECLINE:

The connection between the crisis and the controlled economy:

Heichelheim, F. M. "Welthistorische Geschichtspunkte zu den vormittelalterlichen Wirtschaftsepochen," *Schmollers Jahrbuch,* 56 (1932), 994 ff.; 57 (1933), 1,034 ff.

Leopold, H. M. R. *De Spiegel van het Verleden. Beschouwingen over den Ondergang van het romeinsche Rijk naar Anleiding van het huidige Wereldgebeuren*. Rotterdam, 1918.

Economic causes for the collapse of the empire:

Barbagallo, C. "Il problema della rovina della civiltà antica," *Civiltà moderna* (1933), 508 ff.; *Atti della Accad. Pontaniana,* 63 (1933), 197 ff.

Chapot, V. "Les causes de décadence du monde antique," *Revue de Synthèse* 42 (1926), 83–91.

Rostovtzeff, M. "The Decay of the Ancient World and its Economic Explanations," *Econ. Hist. Review,* 2 (1929–30), 197 ff.

Weber, M. *Gesammelte Aufsätze für Sozial- und Wirtschaftsgeschichte*. Tübingen, 1924, pp. 289 ff.

West, L. C. "The Economic Collapse of the Roman Empire," *Class. Journ.,* 28 (1933), 96 ff.

Westermann, W. L. "The Economic Basis of the Decline of Ancient Culture." *Amer. Hist. Review* 20 (1915), 724 ff.

CONCLUSION

On the end of the economies of the ancient world:

Dopsch, A. *Wirtschaftl. u. soziale Grundlagen der europäischen Kulturentwickelung aus der Zeit von Caesar bis auf karl der Grosse.* 2d ed.; 2 vols. Vienna, 1923–24.

———. *Die Wirtschaftsentwickelung der Karolingerzeit.* 3d ed.; 2 vols. Darmstadt, 1962.

See also:

Lacour-Gayet, J. (ed.) *Histoire du commerce,* Vol. 2. Paris, 1950, pp. 189 ff. (commerce of the Middle Ages is treated by Mme. Boulet-Sautel).

Latouche, R. "De la Gaule romaine à la Gaule franque: aspects sociaux et économiques de l' évolution," in *Settimane di studio del Centro italiano di studi sull' atto Medio Evo,* Vol. 9. Spoletto, 1962, pp. 379–409.

———. *Les origines de l' économie occidentale (4ᵉ–11ᵉ siècles)* ("L'évolution de l'humanité" Series, Vol. 43). Paris, 1956.

Lombard, M. "L'or musulman du 7ᵉ au 11ᵉ siècles," *Annales, Economies, Sociétés, Civilisations* 2 (1947); also "Mahomet et Charlemagne," *ibid.* 3 (1948).

Pettino, A. "Crepuscolo e crollo dell' economia antica," *Bulletin de l' Institut Historique Belge de Rome,* 33 (1961), 165–94.

Pirenne, H. *Mahomet et Charlemagne.* Paris and Brussels, 1937.

Index

Abraham, 17
Actium, battle of, 33
Aegeans, 10
Aegean Sea, 10, 11, 36, 37
Aes rude, 52; *signatum,* 52–53
Africa, 6, 11, 12, 14, 36, 44, 46, 51, 66, 74, 75, 77, 78, 80, 82, 83, 89, 91, 92
Agis, King, 39
Agriculture: Carthaginian, 45, 46; Greek, 28–29; Roman, 66–67, 74 –75, 86; *see also* Crops
Aigina, 20, 25, 30
Akhaians (Achaeans), 10
Akkadians, 9
Alalia (Aleria), battle of, 13, 44
Alexander the Great, 22, 33, 37, 44
Alexandria, 34, 36, 38, 42, 43
Amanus Mountains, 3, 11
Amasis, Pharaoh, 13
Amber, 50
Ammianus Marcellinus, 95
Anachoresis, 43
Anatocism, 26, 58, 64, 95
Ancus Martius, 48
Animals, as money, 16, 52
Antiocheia (Antioch), 34, 37, 63, 91, 92, 95
Antonine emperors, 80
Apameia, 34, 35
Apiculture, 45
Arabia, 6, 36, 79, 101
Arboriculture, 2, 29, 54, 74, 78
Archimedes, 36
Aristotle, 21, 23, 25–26, 31
Arretium, 49, 75, 79
Arsinöe, 34
As, 52, 54, 59
Asia Minor, 13, 18, 27, 34, 37, 38, 66, 78, 85
Asia, Province of, 62
Assyria, 18
Athens, 20, 21, 25, 29, 30, 40, 49, 63; banks, 26–27; business legislation, 23; democracy, 31; economics, 22–23; imports and exports, 24; population, 31; public works, 31; stock exchange, 27
Atlantic Ocean, 6, 12, 44
Attica, 28, 29
Augustus, 68, 72, 74, 77, 81, 83, 87
Aurelian, 87, 96, 97
Aureus, 72, 87
Aventine Hill, 54

Babylon, 4, 9–10, 16, 20, 22, 37
Bactriana (Turkestan), 37
Baltic Sea, 24, 50, 74
Banks and bankers, 21, 38, 42; Athenian, 26–27; Roman, 58, 97; Royal Bank of Egypt, 38, 41
Barter, 15, 24, 89, 103
Bedawi, 7
Berenice, 34
Bitter Lakes, 6
Black Sea (Pontus Euxinus), 10, 13, 25, 37
Boiotia, 39
Britain, 78

Bronze, 17, 87; Age, 48; law, 42; money, 20, 37, 43, 44, 52, 63
Brutus, 64
Bucchero ware, 49
Business: Greek, 28; Roman, 58–59, 80–82; *see also* Guilds; Professions
Businessmen, Roman, 60–61, 63
Byblos, 11

Caesar, Julius, 61, 62, 69, 70
Caius Gracchus, 69, 70
Campania, 49, 67, 75, 85
Canals, 33, 35, 73; Nile–Red Sea, 6, 22, 73
Capital, mobility of, 9–10, 25–27
Capitalism, state, 40–41
Cappadocia, 9
Capua, 59
Caracalla, 72, 87
Carolingian period, 104
Carthage, 11, 33, 43–46, 49, 62, 63; commercial methods, 45; destruction, 46, 66
Carthaginians, 13, 15(n. 2), 20, 24, 49, 50; *see also* Phoenicians
Caspian Sea, 37
Cassiterides Islands, 4, 12
Cassius *(triumvir)*, 60
Cato the Elder, 67, 86
Cattle-raising, 29, 66
Charlemagne, 103
China, 22, 37, 74, 79, 90
Christianity, 85
Cicero, 46, 50, 57, 61, 63, 64, 65, 70
Claudius, 77
Cleruchs, 35, 39, 43; *see also* Colonies, Greek and Phoenician
Cloaca Maxima, 49
Cluvii, 58
Coele-Syria, 34
Coinage, 15, 18–21, 25; Carthaginian, 45; Etruscan, 53; plated, 25; Roman, 53, 59–60, 63, 72, 88; speculation in, 94; standards of, 27, 30; *see also* Money
Colonies: Greek and Phoenician, 10–14; Roman, 51, 56, 57, 62, 65, 70, 75; *see also* Cleruchs; Magna Graecia
Columella, 75
Comana, 35
Commerce, 4–7, 36–38, 72; Roman roads and, 57
Commodus, 72
Comneni emperors, 87
Constantine, 87, 88, 98
Constantinople, 90, 92, 97, 100, 101; *see also* Rome, Eastern Empire
Copper, 3, 4, 17, 37, 47, 49, 87
Corfu, 13
Corinth, 13, 25, 49, 62, 66; Isthmus of, 73
Corsica, 13, 44
Credit, 5, 58, 90; *see also* Interest; Loans; Usury
Crete, Cretans, 5, 10
"Croesids," 19
Croesus, 19, 20
Crops, 36; rotation, 29; *see also* Agriculture
Croton, 13
Cumae, 13; battle of, 50
Cush (Ethiopia), 7
Customs duties: Athenian, 23; Egyptian, 41
Cyprus, 3, 13
Cyrene, 13
Cyrus, 19

Dacia, 72, 79
Danube, 73, 76, 78, 79, 90; army of, 77
Daric, 20
Darius, 6, 20
Debt, 21, 39, 54, 55–56, 68; slavery for nonpayment, 10, 30, 56, 63; *see also* Interest; Loans; Usury
Delos, 37
Delphoi (Delphi), 24, 26
Denarius, 59, 60, 72, 88
Depopulation, 31, 39, 56; *see also* Population
Diocletian, 87, 88
Distribution, 4–7, 14; in Greece, 23–24
Dole, public, 31, 38; Roman, 69, 77–78
Domitian, 76, 79
Dorians, Dorian invasion, 4, 10, 48
Drachma, 17, 25, 30, 37, 38, 53, 60, 88, 89

Ebro River, 44

Economy: agricultural, 2; ancient, 1–7, 71; in classical Greece, 22–32; closed, 2, 86, 103; domestic, 5; early Italian, 47–48; Egyptian, 7–9; forestry, 1; Frankish, 101, 102; Hellenistic, 33–38; monetary, 24; "natural" and nonmonetary, 16, 17; pastoral, 1, 47; post-Etruscan, 50–51; stages of evolution, 4–5; urban, 5, 34; world-wide, 5
Egypt: 1–7 *passim,* 11, 15, 16, 17, 20, 24, 25, 29, 33–38 *passim,* 72, 74, 77, 78, 81, 85, 88–89; engineering constructions, 7–8; pharaohs' state socialism, 40; Royal Bank, 38, 41; state control, 8, 40–43; "supply towns," 8
El Fayum, 8, 35, 43, 85
Elba, 49
Ephesos, 19, 73
Estates, 35, 39, 41, 67, 80, 81, 85, 89, 92, 103
Etruscans, 20, 24, 44, 47, 48, 49, 50, 53
Euboia, 25, 39; Euboic standard *(drachma),* 25, 30
Eupatridae, 29, 30
Euphrates, 6, 36–37, 73
Exchange, 4–7, 41, 96

Family ownership, 2
Foreigners, 26, 57, 58, 60
Frankish period, 102
Freedmen, 60
Fruit trees; *see* Arboriculture

Gabinius, 61
Gallia Narbonensis, 63
Gaul, Gauls, 4, 14, 24, 50, 52, 53, 54, 62, 66, 75, 76, 78, 83, 91, 101, 102, 104; river axes, 73
Gaza, 25
Germans, Germany, 74, 75, 78
Glass, 12, 45
Gold, 17, 25, 45, 61, 103; Roman coinage, 59–60, 63, 72, 88
Grain, 2, 16, 23, 27, 37, 54; *see also* Wheat
Greece, 1, 2, 4, 19, 22, 33, 43, 83, 85; cities, 30, 77; classical economy, 22–32; decline, 38–40, 78, 79; Hellenistic era, 33–40; Roman conquest, 46; social problems, 29–32
Greeks, 1, 2, 16, 17, 20, 43, 44, 49, 50; of Asia, 17; expansion, 10–14, 34–38; exploration by, 12
Guilds, 49, 83, 103–4; early Roman, 48; *see also* Business; Professions

Hadrian, 81
Hanno, 12
Harbors, 51, 57, 73
Herodotus, 15(n. 2), 18
Hiero II (Hieron), 63
Himera, battle of, 44
Hippalos, 36
Hiram, king of Tyre, 12
Hittites, 5, 7
Honorius, 85
Horse, 5, 45
Hyksos, 4, 5

Iberians, 14
Iliad, 1, 4, 15(n. 2), 16
India, 6, 36, 74, 79
Indo-Europeans, 5, 48
Industry, 14, 39; Etruscan, 49; Greek, 28; Italian, 67, kinds of, 3–4; Roman, 75–76
Insurance, 26
Interest, 25–26, 55, 68; in Babylon, 10; compound, *see* Anatocism; in Greece, 26; *see also* Debt; Loan; Usury
Iron, 4, 17, 27, 28, 41, 49; Age, 48
Isocrates, 31
Italy, 13, 37, 46, 54, 66, 76, 78, 83, 85, 91, 104; depopulation, 56; foreign money in, 53; pre- and early Roman economy, 47–56

Jerusalem, 17
Jews, 73, 103
Joint stock company, 26
Jugera, 54
Jugurtha, 60
Julian, 95
Juno Moneta, temple of, 59
Jus gentium, 58
Justinian, 84, 95, 96, 99
Juvenal, 79

Kerasunde, 66
Kikkar, 9, 52
Kleomenes, 36
Koptos, 36

Labor: forces, 96, 97; free, 35, 42; manual, 4, 80; tenant, 82–83, 86; *see also* Slaves and slavery
Lactantius, 95
Lagid rulers, 40
Lake Moeris, 8, 36
Land distribution, 39, 69
Laodikeia, 34
Latifundia; see Estates
Latins, 50
Latium, 49
Laurion (Laurium) mines, 24, 25, 26, 39
Law: commercial, 23; Greek, 58; maritime, 37; Roman, 54, 55, 57–59, 65, 68–70, 80–81, 94, 97–98
Lead, 49, 87
Lebanon, 3, 11
Letter of credit, 27
Lex: Claudia, 60; Genucia, 55; Marcia, 55; Poetelia Papiria, 56; *Sempronia agraria,* 69; *Sempronia frumentaria,* 69
Libya, 13
Lighthouse, 36, 73
Ligurians, 14
Livy (Titus Livius), 50
Loans, 26, 27, 38, 41, 55, 58, 68; *see also* Credit; Debt; Interest; Usury
Lucullus, 66
Lydians, 19

Macedonia, Macedonians, 25, 35, 46, 62
Magna Graecia, 13, 14, 25, 46, 49, 51–52, 53, 59, 78
Mago, 45
Malacca, 74
Marcus Aurelius, 72, 74
Marius, 70
Markets, 28, 48, 57
Massilia, 13, 20, 60
Mediterranean Sea, 6, 11, 13, 44, 73, 78, 101–2
Memphis, 11
Mercantilism, 42
Merovingian period, 101, 102, 104
Mesopotamia, 1, 3, 5, 6, 7, 9, 17, 34
Metal, stamped, 18; *see also* Minerals; names of metals
Metallurgy, 12, 28, 49, 67
Metalworking, 3, 76
Metic; *see* Foreigners
Middlemen, 9
Migrations, 2
Miletos, 19
Military expeditions, as trade, 7
Mina, 9, 17
Minerals, 3, 5, 23, 24; *see also* Metal
Mines, 4, 7, 24, 25, 41, 45, 76, 79, 81, 82
Misthophoria, 31
Mithridates, 62
Modena, 76
Monarchy, absolute, 34
Money, 37–38, 44; and crisis, 21, 43; devaluation, 21, 25, 38, 43, 59, 80, 88; fiduciary, 21; invention of, 18–19, 21; in Italy, 51–53; legal consequences of, 21; minting of, 24; nominal, 14, 15–16; nonmetallic, 16; real, 14, 15; savings, 15; spread of, 19–20; standards, 25, 37, 87; weighted metal as, 52; *see also* Coinage
Monopolies, state, 41, 81, 96
Monsoon, 36
Mt. Pangaios, 25
Mule, 2
Murashu family, 9(n.1)
Myceneans, 10

Naucratis, 13
Navigation, 11, 36; *see also* Transportation, maritime
Neapolis, 53
Necho (Necoh), Pharaoh, 6, 12
Negroes, African, 15(n.2)
Nero, 72, 80, 81
Nerva, 80
Nile, 6, 22, 36, 73
Noricum, 61
Note of hand, 38
Numa, 48, 50
Numidia, 60

Obol, 17
Odyssey, 11
Oil, 24, 29, 34, 41, 43, 73, 102
Oil-grain seeds, 2, 41
Oliganthropia, 31, 39
Olive, 2, 29, 49
Ophir, 12
Ore extraction, 35
Ostia, 48, 51, 73, 77
Ounce (*uncia*), 52, 53
Ownership, private, 35
Oxen, 2, 5

Pactolos River, 19
Palermo, 44
Palestine, 2
Palladius, 86
Paris, 103
Partnership: business, 26; limited, 10
Pasagardae, 20
Pasion bank (Athens), 26
Peloponnesian War, 31
Peloponnesus, 25
Pergamum, 65
Pericles, 29
Persepolis, 20
Persia, 34, 37, 74, 90, 96
Persian Empire, 22, 24, 29
Persian Gulf, 6, 37
Pessinonte, 35
Pharos, 36
Philadelphia, 34
Philip (Macedonian coin), 25
Phrygians, 10
Phocaeans (Phokaians), Phocaea, 13, 19
Phoenicians, 1, 15; expansion, 10–14; *see also* Carthage; Carthaginians
Piracy, 35, 37, 49, 89; Phoenician, 11; as trade, 7
Piraeus, 23, 27, 39
Plato, 32
Pliny the Younger, 67, 79, 82
Plough, 2
Polybios, 44
Pompey the Great, 57, 65
Pontine marshes, 48, 79
Pontus Euxinus: *see* Black Sea
Population, 29, 31; *see also* Depopulation
Po River, 49
Ports: *see* Harbors
Portugal, 81
Pound (*libra*), 52, 59
Poverty, agrarian, 39
Prices, fixed, 41
Production, 27–29, 41, 42, 76; expansion in Hellenistic period, 34–36; over-, 28
Professions, 35; organization of, 96–98; *see also* Business; Guilds
Ptolemais, 34
Ptolemies, 37, 40; Ptolemy Auletes, 61; Ptolemy II Philadelphus, 35, 36, 42
Publicans, 59, 64, 71, 82
Pump, suction and piston, 36
Punic Wars, 44–45, 59
Purple, 12, 90, 96
Pytheas, 37

Rabirius Postumus, 61
Ravenna, 90
Red Sea, 6, 22, 36
Revolution: agrarian, 66; economic, 14; "first industrial," 3
Rhine, 73, 75, 76, 78, 79, 90
Rhodes, 37, 38, 51, 58
Rivers, 6, 73; *see also under* names of rivers
Roads: Etruscan, 49; Roman, 51, 56–57, 73–74
Romans, 16, 20, 35, 37, 44, 45, 46
Rome, 21, 44; agrarian measures, 54, 80; colonies, 51, 56, 57, 62, 65, 70, 75, commerce, 60–61, 73–74; conquests, 61–66; early history, 47–51; Eastern Empire, 84–100 *passim;* economic crises, 66–68, 84–92; fall, 99; feudalism, 91; food supply, 97 (*see also* Dole); Forum, 49, 50; imbalances, 76–80; invasions, 84; monetary stability, 72; Senate, 46, 79, 87; social crises, 53–56, 68–70; state budget, 65; state control, 81–82, 92–100; towns of Empire, 92, 103; unemployment, 68–70
Romulus, 48
Rutilius Namatianus, 89
Rutilius Rufus, 65

Saguntum, 45
St. Cyprian, 81
St. John Chrysostom, 92
St. Melania, 91
St. Paul, 57
Salamis, 63
Samos, 28
Sancta Sophia, 100
Sardinia, 44, 51
Sardis, 19, 22
Scaptius, 64
Scillies, 4
Scipio Aemilianus, 45
Scythia, Scythians, 14, 24, 74, 77
Seisachtheia edict, 30
Seleukia, 34, 36, 37
Seleukid kingdom, 34, 35, 38, 46
Servian wall, 49
Servius Tullius, 49, 50, 52
Sestertius, 59, 72, 88
Severan dynasty, 80; Severus Alexander, 96; Septimius Severus, 96
Shat, 16
Shekel, 9, 17; Median, 20
Sicily, 12, 13, 20, 44, 45, 51, 63, 65–66, 74, 77, 78; *see also* Magna Graecia
Sidon, 11
Silk, 22, 74, 79, 84, 90, 96
Silver, 17, 25, 37, 39, 44, 49, 63, 88, 103
Sinai peninsula, 3, 7
Slaves and slavery, 4, 5, 7, 11, 23, 34, 35, 49, 57, 60, 67, 69, 75, 81, 82, 86; markets, 37; *see also* Debt; Labor
Slumps, 28, 66, 96
Solidus, 87, 88
Solomon, King, 12
Solon, 26, 30
Spain, 44, 45, 66, 74, 76, 78
Sparta, 17, 30, 39
Speculation, 27, 36, 61; in coins, 94
Stater, 17
Stock-raising; *see* Cattle-raising; Economy, pastoral
Strabo, 34, 73
Straits of Messina, 13
Suez, isthmus of, 6, 36
Sulla, 59, 62, 68, 70
Sumerians, 9
Susa, 3, 20, 22
Sybaris, 13
Syracuse, 13, 24, 29, 32, 44, 50
Syria, 35, 75, 85, 90

Tacitus, 78
Takhos, Pharaoh, 20
Talent, 9, 17, 52
Tanagra, 39
Tarentine War, 46
Tarentum, 13, 51, 53, 57, 66
Tarquin the Elder, 49
Tarquinius Superbus, 50
Tarshish (Tartessos) (southern Spain), 6, 11, 13
Taxes, 41, 63, 67, 82, 89, 91, 94, 103; tax farmers; *see* Publicans
Techniques, agricultural, 2–3
Technology, industrial, 4; *see also* Industry; Metallurgy; Metalworking
Terramara period, 47–48
Thales of Miletos, 27
Theodosius, 88
Thessaly, 39
Thrace, 25
Thule, 37
Tiber, 50, 57, 77
Tiberius, 68, 79
Tiberius Gracchus, 67, 69–70
Tigris, 6, 36
Tin, 3–4, 12, 87
Trade: agencies, 13; balance of, 67–68; Carthaginian monopoly of, 44; early Roman, 48; Etruscan, 49; with Far East, 79–80; in foodstuffs, 5, 24; international, 5, 7; land, 12; large-scale, 21; late Roman, 103; local, 5; Phoenician, 11; routes, 24, 36–37
Trajan, 72, 73, 74, 79, 80, 81
Transformations, 28; within early Roman Empire, 80–83
Transit depots, 37
Transportation, 3, 5–6, 36–37; of heavy goods, 14, 23; land, 6, 23, 56; maritime, 23, 57, 73; *see also* Navigation
Triens, 88
Tripolitania, 96
Trojan War, 10
Tuscany, 49, 85
Tyre, 11, 44

Tyrrhenian Sea (Mare Tyrrhenium), 49

Ugarit, 11
Ukraine, 24, 66, 74
Unemployment, 39; *see also under* Rome
Ur, 18
Usury, 55, 90, 95; *see also* Interest; Loans

Valentinian, 97
Valerian, 87
Vandals, 89
Verres, 63, 65
Vespasian, 73, 75, 78
Villanova, 48
Vine, 2, 29, 34, 63, 103
Vipasca mine, 81
Visigoths, 84, 99

Water mill, 36, 75
Wheat, 29, 38, 43, 46, 63, 66, 67, 69, 73, 74, 76, 77, 78, 88; *see also* Grain
Wine, 24, 29, 73, 103
Works, public, 35, 71, 73, 77, 81
Worm screw, 36

Xenophon, 28
Xerxes, 27

Zama, battle of, 46